An Intelligent Person's Guide to Fascism

An Intelligent Person's Guide to Fascism

RICHARD GRIFFITHS

Duckworth

First published in 2000 by
Gerald Duckworth & Co. Ltd
61 Frith Street, London W1D 3JL
Tel: 020 7434 4242
Fax: 020 7434 4420
Email: enquiries@duckworth-publishers.co.uk
www.ducknet.co.uk

A catalogue record for this book is available
from the British Library

ISBN 0 7156 2918 2

Typeset by
Derek Doyle & Associates, Liverpool
Printed in Great Britain by
Biddles Limited, www.biddles.co.uk

To the memory of all who suffered
at the hands of those described in this book

Contents

Preface

There are few greater challenges than that of being asked to write a general book, for a widely diverse audience, about a subject that has already received a great deal of critical attention. On the other hand, it gives one an opportunity to think adventurously, and for once to escape from the enclosed vision of those aspects on which one has almost too much information to reach a reasonable overall picture. In the process of writing this book, it has become clear that some of the concerns which have bedevilled scholars working on this subject have been at best irrelevant, and at worst misleading.

There has, of course, been a great deal of good work done on the subject of 'fascism', and I am indebted to the work of a good number of scholars, whose writings are listed in the Bibliography. I would like, however, to single out those that I have found most useful: Roger Griffin's *Fascism*, which tellingly brings together examples of the speeches and writings of fascists from a wide variety of nations and movements; Roger Eatwell's *Fascism: a History*, particularly valuable on Italy and Germany; Zeev Sternhell's two outstanding books on the French radical Right; Eugen Weber's definitive *Action Française*; Philip Rees's *Biographical Dictionary of the Extreme Right since 1890*, an invaluable source on individual fascists; and a number of remarkable collective volumes, including Martin Blinkhorn's *Fascists and Conservatives*, Rogger and Weber's *The European Right: A Historical Profile*, Stuart Woolf's *European Fascism*, and Cheles, Ferguson and Vaughan's *The Far Right in Western and Eastern Europe*.

Many people have helped me, over the years, in discussion of the issues involved. In the nineteen-sixties and nineteen-seventies, I had a number of useful conversations with Henri Massis and Sir Charles Petrie (both of whom figure in this book), and with Robert Aron, Colonel Alan Dower, René Gillouin, Léon Poliakov, General Max von Viebahn and Monsieur Voisin (the Action Française bookseller in the Rue de la Sorbonne). Others with whom I have had fruitful discussions at various times, or jointly participated in specialist conferences, have been: Geoffrey Alderman, Vernon Bogdanor, Manuel Braga da Cruz, John Butt, Manuel Cabral, Luciano Cheles, David Childs, Antonio Costa Pinto, Maurice Cowling, Roger Eatwell, Gino Gamberini, Maurice de Gandillac, Julie Gottlieb, the late Henri Gouhier, Roger Griffin, Nick Hewitt, Christopher Husbands, Julian Jackson, Jeremy Jennings, Douglas Johnson, Cécile Laborde, Eduardo Lourenço, Manuel de Lucena, Helder Macedo, Kenneth Minogue, the late Peter Morris, Tom Nevin, Scott Newton, Stanley Payne, Michael Pinto-Duschinsky, Luis de Sousa Rebelo, Pierre Roland-Lévy, Stefan Schreiner, Peter Stead, Dan Stone, Rob Stradling, Richard Thurlow, Shirley Vinall, Richard Vinen, Donald Cameron Watt, Paul Wilkinson and Jim Wolfreys.

I also wish to thank to Robin Baird-Smith of Duckworth's, who commissioned this book, and Martin Rynja, who has seen it through to completion.

Introduction

'Fascism'* is probably the most misused, and over-used, word of our times. Even the most 'intelligent persons' have been known to use it without considering its implications.

Throughout the second half of the twentieth century, it has been in constant use, mainly as a term of abuse. It can be used indiscriminately to describe anything of which one disapproves. Indeed, both sides in a dispute may use the same word to describe their enemies. From differing points of view, the IRA, the Royal Ulster Constabulary, Robert Mugabe, Lady Thatcher, Slobodan Milosevic, President Clinton, the *Daily Telegraph*, Sir Winston Churchill, General de Gaulle, the Tate Modern, Opus Dei, New Labour, Old Labour, certain university Vice-Chancellors (and their opponents), a wide variety of publicans, and even the Pope, have all at one time or other been described as 'fascist'. New concepts, such as 'designer fascism', 'cyber-fascism', or 'euro-fascism' are continually emerging.

In this modern use, the word does of course have certain overtones. These can relate to authoritarianism, to 'control freakery'; they can in other circumstances imply violence, extremism, or racism; or the term can merely be applied to the political Right in general (this last being a gross over-simplification, given the left-wing characteristics to be found in most varieties of fascism). A wide range of other attributes, however, made up 'fascism' as it existed at the time of the term's original use, in the inter-war period; and the more restricted attributes ascribed to it in our

---

* As, throughout this book, we shall continually be needing to distinguish between the general idea of 'fascism', and the specific movement from which it stemmed, Italian Fascism, we shall be using a well-established technique that is possible in English (but not, for example, in French), by putting the first letter of the former in lower case (except at the beginning of sentences), and using a capital letter for the latter.

own time are in fact applicable to a wide range of other political movements, and are not specific to 'fascism'.

Yet are people wrong, nowadays, to use this word in the ways in which they do? Words can change their meaning, as years pass, and the creators of dictionaries tend merely to note that the word now means something different from its original meaning. The word 'defeatism', for example, meant, when it was coined in Russia during the First World War, the aim of bringing about the defeat of one's own side, for internal political ends ('revolutionary defeatism'). By the end of the war, however, it had come to mean, in France and Britain, something quite different: an attitude of pessimistic acceptance of the possibility of defeat. It is this second meaning that is now widely accepted, and we do not bemoan the fact that the original meaning has been lost. Why should we deplore, therefore, any changes that have occurred in the use of the word 'fascism'? Why should we not accept that it is as useful as a catch-all term of abuse as words like 'bastard' or 'bugger' are (most people described by these terms of abuse being neither born out of wedlock, nor homosexual).

It is, of course, futile to deplore new usages; language does change, and words can always be useful, however they have been transformed, so long as their context is understood. If 'fascism' were *merely* used as a simplified modern term of abuse, all would be straightforward. We could just continue applying it indiscriminately to everyone we disliked. But 'fascism' is a more important word than that. It is a word which, in the history of the twentieth century, is intimately connected with some of the most terrible events that have taken place, events which still cast their shadow over us today. We owe it to ourselves to have a clearer picture of what it means, and what it has meant. Only thus will we be able fully to understand our own times.

Many historians and political scientists have set out to provide this clearer picture. The only problem is, that the picture they have provided has sometimes been *too* clear. Their desire to provide all-embracing definitions has obscured the complex and often contradictory nature of reality, which is difficult to grasp except by using a discourse full of qualifications, provisos, reservations, and exceptions.

The definitions are often alarmingly precise: for some, 'Fascism is definable as an ideology with a specific "positive" utopian vision of the ideal state of society'; for others, it is 'a synthesis of organic nationalism and anti-Marxist socialism'; for others again, 'a combination of mass revolutionist strategies with reactionary ideologies compounded of virulent ultra-nationalism, exaltation of irrationality, illegality, violence and fanatical anti-communism'. Most commentators seem to agree 'on the importance of defining fascism', although this usually means cutting out of one's definition some people who have always been believed to be fascists, but who now have to be described as 'not *really* fascists, though (...) they have frequently been accused of being fascist', because they do not fit the arbitrary definition that has just been provided.

The difficulty is not, of course, confined to 'fascism'. Such definitions are as difficult to make in literature or philosophy as they are in politics. Wittgenstein's theories on the subject of definition are relevant here. Every definition we make is unsatisfactory either because it is too narrow (and exceptions can be found to it), or because it is too wide (and many examples of similar cases can be contained within it, which are clearly different from the subject you are attempting to define). For these reasons one has never in literature, for example, been able to come to a satisfactory definition of Tragedy. No definition could cover everything which is commonly believed to deserve the name of a 'tragedy'. All one needs to do, to prove this, is try to put together Greek tragedy, Spanish Renaissance tragedy, Italian and French Renaissance tragedy, Shakespeare's tragedies, French seventeenth-century tragedy, English Restoration tragedy, and so on. All one can say, eventually, is that Tragedy was perceived to be like this in one country at one specific time, and like that in another country at another time.

Fascism presents just such a situation. All one needs to do is take, one by one, the attributes most usually ascribed to it, and see how they fare in relation to Wittgenstein's criteria:

'*Totalitarian*': too wide, applicable to all kinds of other movements as well.

'*Racist, anti-Semitic*': too narrow, in that certain movements commonly accepted as fascist were not racist; yet too wide, because it is applicable to other movements as well (including movements of the late nineteenth-century Left, and, of course, twentieth-century Communism).

'*Nationalist*': too wide, applicable to many other kinds of
    movement.
'*Populist*': too wide, applicable to other movements.
'*Anti-capitalist*': too wide, applicable to other movements.
'*Reactionary*': misleading, and in many cases untrue.
'*Use of mass myths*': too wide.
'*Utopian*': too narrow, and at the same time too wide.
'*Pagan*': too narrow; witness the existence of 'Catholic
    fascism'.
'*Cult of Violence*': too wide, applicable to other movements.

Thus, despite the protestations of some theorists of fascism, one
feels bound to subscribe to the view expressed by Milza and
Bernstein that 'No universally accepted definition of the fascist
phenomenon exists, no consensus, however slight, as to its range,
its ideological origins, or the modalities of action which charac-
terise it'.[1] Krejci has rightly noted of fascism that 'the generic
usage of any term cannot take into account all variations which
necessarily appear both between countries and over time'.[2] This is
not, of course, to say that all the elements we have been
mentioning are not present, in various cocktail mixes, in the
various forms of fascism, and that it will not be worth our looking,
among other things, at the presence of these various factors.
    If, as is sometimes useful, one were to try to define fascism by
what it is *not*, the most obvious opposite to it would be 'conservatism' with a small 'c'. Fascism, in theory, and when in
opposition, was essentially a revolutionary movement, wishing to
re-order society on a new and different basis (as opposed to
'conservatively' trying to retain existing structures, or even to
return to traditional structures that have disappeared). Even
here, however, the generalisation would not stand up, as, when
fascism has come to power (and often while still out of power), its
leaders have very often compromised with the more conservative
elements in society. One of the main problems we will be examining is the difference between fascism in opposition, and fascism
in power; and also the relationship (often tenuous) between
fascist theory and fascist practice. The revolutionary, anti-capitalist aspect of fascism was strongest in those movements which
did not come to power, or in movements like Nazism and Italian
Fascism *before* they came to power.

Dictionaries, of course, have to produce simple, clear definitions of words, and it is fascinating to note that the *Shorter Oxford English Dictionary*, faced with the word 'fascism', has craftily shelved the problem by taking the word merely to refer to Mussolini's Italian movement, from which international fascism took its name:

> **Fascist**. 1921 [ad. It. *fascista*, f. *fascio* group.] One of a body of Italian nationalists organised in 1919 under Benito Mussolini to oppose Bolshevism. Hence **Fascism**, their principles and organisation.

It would solve many problems, but be seriously misleading, to base our study of European fascism, in this way, purely upon the Italian experiment. While it will of course be essential for us to look at Italy, for the origin of many policies and attitudes, and for the charisma it gave to the word fascism, it will in fact be only a minor part of our concerns.

In politics, an even more intractable problem than that of fascism is, intimately bound up with it, that of Left and Right. Most of the attributes which are cited for each are capable of being ascribed, in certain circumstances, to the other, and a politician's stance can often be impossible to relate definitively to one or to the other. The story is told of a young lecturer who agreed to lecture on an MA course on 'Literature and Commitment in France, 1870-1940'. It was his task to lecture on the writers of the Right, while someone else lectured on the writers of the Left. At his first class, he told the students the authors he would be dealing with: Péguy, Sorel, Drieu la Rochelle, Malraux, etc. The students were amazed: at least half of those he had mentioned were on the reading-list of the person lecturing on the Left!

If Left and Right are at times difficult to distinguish from each other (and nowhere more so than in fascism), within the Right itself it is even more difficult to perceive the characteristics that can infallibly distinguish the various categories. Theoretical distinctions have continually been made between 'conservatism' (in the continental sense) and 'fascism'; but (as mentioned) practical reality consists of nuances, alliances, political arrangements, in which such distinctions have little place, and in which men use the means, and the men, that are available to them. Much of the time people involved in contemporary events have no thought of ideas and doctrines, or of there being any contradictory elements in the alliances they are forging.

It is too easy to see the past as providing satisfactory patterns. We tend to see things from on high; we think we can distinguish clearly between the programmes, the theories, and the characteristics of different manifestations of the Right. But at the time when fascism was being fashioned, all was not so clear. Like Stendhal's hero Fabrice, in *La Chartreuse de Parme* (who took part in the Battle of Waterloo without any conception of what was actually happening in the battle), most of those who got mixed up in politics in the inter-war period, even the most important of them, could not see things as clearly as we, the armchair politicians, think we can. The distinction between 'conservatism' and 'fascism' was on the whole absent from their minds. Those whom the political scientists would like to class as 'conservatives' often thought of themselves as 'fascists', and vice versa. Alliances were based on political reality rather than political theory, and the vision of the nature of the contemporary political world was often governed by wishful thinking rather than by the clear conceptions that political scientists would like to see.

In these circumstances, it would be tempting to take the attitude I did when on a Welsh Arts Council Committee to choose the best Welsh English-language book of the year. What was the definition of a Welsh book? Something written on a Welsh subject by any author, or something written by a Welsh author? And who was a Welsh author? Someone who was of Welsh origin, living in Wales? Someone of Welsh origin, living outside Wales? Someone of non-Welsh origin, living in Wales? And what was the definition of 'of Welsh origin'? (One didn't quite get into the question, on the model of the Nazi racial laws, of how many Welsh grandparents one had to have – but one was not far from doing so). Eventually, in desperation, I decided that anyone who *believed* him- or herself to be Welsh *was* Welsh.

It would thus be tempting to say that anyone, between the wars, who believed himself to be fascist, was fascist; or that anyone who was believed to be fascist by others, was fascist. But that, too, would be too simple. Fascism can be depicted neither purely by global retrospective definitions, nor purely by contemporary perceptions. There is, however, a balance between the two which can be illuminating. People's contemporary views as to what 'fascism' was, can tell us a lot not only about the nature of the beast, but also about the changes which took place as the inter-war period progressed. Many people, by the late Thirties, saw all the diverse movements in the different nations of Europe as being 'fascist', and as being part of a great new political departure (whether they enthusiastically hailed it, or proclaimed its dangers). This belief is something with which it is important for us to get to grips if we wish to understand one of the driving forces of our century; and in order to get to grips with it, we will need to look at it historically, bearing in mind all the complexities as we do so.

This book will therefore be an attempt to pin down the elusive, and to examine the whole phenomenon of fascism both as it was and as it was perceived, in order to try to understand more fully the complex reality that dominated European life and politics in the Thirties, and which still has repercussions on our life today.

1. P. Milza et S. Bernstein, *Dictionnaire historique des fascismes et du nazisme*, Brussels, 1992, p. 7.
2. Jaroslav Krejci, 'Introduction: Concepts of Right and Left', in *Neo-Fascism in Europe*, ed. Cheles, Ferguson and Vaughan, London, Longman, 1991, p. 1.

Part One

PRELUDE, 1880-1930

1

Neither Right nor Left

Pre-Fascism

'Fascism', as a concept, was a product of the early nineteen-twenties. The prestige of Mussolini's Italian experiment led for the next 20 years to emulation throughout Europe. It is rarely realised, however, that the reason it did so was that it struck a chord on instruments that were already in existence, and that, because of that, movements in other countries could attach the name, and the symbols, of fascism to their already formed concerns. In this respect, Italian Fascism was not so much the creator of a tradition, as one manifestation, albeit a particularly successful one, of a series of concerns that were in the air.

Already, by the late nineteenth century, various political attitudes had been emerging which the old concepts of Left and Right proved inadequate to describe. Commentators have tended to use such words as 'radical Right' or 'revolutionary Right' to describe them; but even these terms beg the question by continuing to use the word Right as though it were unquestionable. Sternhell's description of fascism as being 'neither Right nor Left' is a useful starting-point for describing these earlier movements, as well as the fascism which succeeded them.

Before exploring these manifestations of a new political outlook, we need to look at the ideological bases and philosophical attitudes which underlay them.

(a) Intellectual bases

Anti-rationalism, and relativism

These political manifestations were in part the product of an atmosphere, in the late nineteenth century, in which all the old certainties were being questioned – not just religion, but also the new religion, that of Science, that had, for a time, seemed so triumphantly to replace the old. Science was seen to have answered none of the fundamental questions facing mankind; and the cult of Reason, which had formed the basis for human ideas of progress ever since the eighteenth century, was similarly seen to have been devalued. Thus occurred, in the last decades of the nineteenth century, what has been called the 'Flight from Reason'.

The philosopher who most neatly sums up this tendency is the Frenchman Bergson (1859-1941). Alongside his revolutionary views on time, change, and memory, Bergson developed a theory of human knowledge which was to have a great influence on his generation. In his view, the language we use, and our methods of analysis, deform what we wish to describe, because they attempt to create a specific and unchanging truth, whereas all things are in continual flux. In these circumstances, we have to rely, for our concepts of the truth, on our intuition; only that, and our reflections on what it reveals to us, come anywhere near to revealing the reality of 'real duration'. In Bergson's system, therefore, human reason was devalued in favour of intuition.

Bergson was a pure philosopher and would have been amazed to find his philosophy quoted as a source for a series of political attitudes; but a number of political thinkers, and in particular Georges Sorel, traced their ideas to his influence. But Bergson was not the sole influence; his philosophy was a particularly well-expressed and well-formulated example of ideas that had already been circulating in the late nineteenth century, in Europe as a whole. In France, the physiologist Jules Soury had been arriving, independently, at a devaluation of the human intelligence, and a corresponding justification of the value of human intuition (and had been, unlike Bergson, drawing political conclusions from this); and in Germany Friedrich Nietzsche had been proclaiming not merely the 'death of God' but also the value of the irrational.

Soury's theories were ostensibly based on his physiological research. They ended up pronouncing the futility of Science, and of rational attempts at knowledge. Man is like the other animals; he can never *know*. All concepts are relative: 'What is truth? And what is science? ... They are views on which men have come to agreement. They are nothing but an *entente* [understanding, or agreement] to which minds have come.'[1]

Friedrich Nietzsche (1844-1900) undermined, in his work from the 1880s onwards, conventional ideas of morality. His philosophy lay, in the words of the title of one of his books, 'beyond good and evil'. Nietzsche condemned the traditional moral values taught by philosophy as being illusory, and moreover pernicious to a satisfying human existence. There is no instinct for these things, he says; on the other hand, there does exist another more important instinct: the will to power, and to a higher, stronger existence. For each individual, that 'will to power' can define, by its usefulness or otherwise, what is moral or desirable. These are therefore not fixed values, but relative ones (and we shall see, not just with Soury and Nietzsche, just how important this concept of 'the relative' was to become in the period, and how closely it affected political attitudes). The values of an age reflect its health or sickness. The values of our own time, he said, are sick ones, born of the Judaeo-Christian system of values, and its most recent forms humanism and socialism, which have corrupted a master morality into a slave morality. The only escape, if the 'meek and poor in spirit' are not to prevail, is to make sure that mankind's fate is governed by the success of its highest types. New men must be developed, supermen, who can put into effect these new values. Struggle is essential for the healthiness of the human race. At times of crisis a 'Superman', an exceptional man of destiny, will arise to put things to rights.

Relating this philosophy to the political field, Nietzsche saw democracy as the most typical example of the Judaeo-Christian slave mentality. But he saw hope ahead:

> Looking at the European of today gives me a great deal of hope: an audacious ruling race is arising. [...] From now on there will be favourable conditions for more extensive power structures, of a kind that have never yet existed. And that is not the most important thing; it has become possible for international groups of the same species to arise, which set themselves the task of raising a *Herren-Rasse* (a race of masters), the future 'lords of the earth'.[2]

Nietzsche's cult of the superman was to have incalculable effect not only on European thought but also on European politics.

The other major thinker to achieve a similar effect was the

Frenchman Georges Sorel (1847-1922), who in 1908, in his *Reflections on Violence (Réflexions sur la violence)*, turned French political thinking on its head. Sorel is one of those people whom it is impossible to classify as either of the Right or of the Left. A convinced anarcho-syndicalist, he found himself, in the years immediately before the First World War, often closely allied with the French extra-parliamentary Right – and this was not just because of certain shared dislikes. Sorel was influenced both by Bergson and by Nietzsche. He shared Bergson's mistrust of the rational, and his belief in intuition; and he echoed Nietzsche's desire for a healthy society, based on a new set of values. A healthy society, for Sorel, was one of conflict. The modern concern for arbitration and peace-making, as opposed to social conflict, had been caused by 'a cowardly middle class' which 'continues to pursue the chimera of social peace'. Violence was important in itself, whether it pursued a practical end or not. The violent act was useful as providing the 'extreme moments' which sustained the class struggle and through that the health and vigour of society as a whole. Progress, humanitarianism, etc., were bourgeois myths which merely helped to sustain a weak and illusory semblance of society. What the proletariat needed were powerful 'myths' that would stir them to action. The reality or otherwise of these myths was of no importance. Thus the 'myth of the general strike' could be a useful spur; but Sorel was a pessimist who did not actually believe in the possibility of success in such a venture; rather, the struggle must become an end in itself.

One of the most striking characteristics of Sorel's philosophy was his basic contempt for the masses, who could be so easily mobilised by often illusory 'myths'. We will find a similar contempt expressed in the structures of the 'radical Right' and of fascism (but also those of Soviet communism), where, unlike those of democrats, socialists or anarchists, there is so little trust in the capability of the masses to run their own affairs that auto-cratic rulers are essential.

Sorel's importance in the eventual development of Italian Fascism was stressed by Mussolini himself, in the article 'Fascism' in the *Enciclopedia Italiana*. The ambivalence of Sorel's position is shown, however, by the fact that he has often been quoted as having had impact on Lenin as well. Such an

equivocal political writer (neither Right nor Left) is perhaps the
most suitable person to stand as a precursor of that most equivocal of political creeds, fascism.

Anti-capitalism and Corporatism

A dislike for the bourgeois capitalist society had been one aspect
of the traditional Right, and particularly the Catholic Right,
during the course of the nineteenth century. It was often based
on unreal premisses. First, an idealistic vision of the healthiness
of the old paternalist agrarian society, where people had known
their place, and aristocrats had known their duties towards those
beneath them as well as their rights. ('The rich man in his castle,
/ the poor man at his gate, / God made them high and lowly, / and
ordered their estate'). Secondly, a belief that, by tearing people
away from the God-fearing rural societies, capitalism had created
a mass of inferior beings without faith or morals. There was also
the more straightforwardly self-interested perception that the
capitalist society of the industrial revolution had produced a
more powerful middle class, and reduced the power of the
nobility. For all these reasons, the traditional Right could express
abhorrence of the new industrial capitalist society; but there was
precious little real concern for the workers in all this.

As the nineteenth century developed, however, a more radical
strain of anti-capitalism came to be found in Right-wing circles,
based on a desire to go, not back to the pre-industrial feudal
society, but forward to a new vision of society in which the lot of
the workers could be ameliorated, and their rights protected. The
hatred of capitalism, in this new form of belief, was still very
strong; it was seen, in its present form, as being destructive of
society, and governed by selfish forces bent on their own individual gain as opposed to the good of the whole. The 'dictatorship
of money' had to be destroyed, and with it the class warfare that
it had engendered.

Though the expression of such views was often extreme and
negative, an important strand of thought developed in the course
of the nineteenth century, which attempted to find practical solutions to what were seen to be society's problems. This was to
become known as 'corporatism'. In its original form, this theory
modelled itself on the medieval guilds, where there was a close

relationship between master and worker – in other words, trades unions to which employers and employed could both belong. In France, the sociologist Frédéric Le Play (1806-82) refined on this theme, extending it to the national level. He saw the family, and a stable family life, as one of the essential conditions for a well-ordered society, and he saw the state as needing to be like just such a well-ordered family. Believing social reform to be not only an economic but also a moral matter, and trusting in man's sense of duty, he based his whole social theory upon a return to a feudal organisation of industrial society. As opposed to the conflict between employers and trades unions, in this new society employers and workers would together be organised into 'corporations' in which they could work together for the common good. Le Play's remedy for the bourgeois exploitation of the proletariat was therefore not a levelling, but a Christian paternalist society in which all classes would realise their duties as well as their rights.

This essentially paternalistic, unreal set of theories was remarkably influential among movements of the Right; but by the twentieth century a far more sophisticated series of structures for a corporatist society were to emerge, covering the whole of a state's activities, including methods of representation in government (whereby people obtained seats according to their role in society, as opposed to democratic votes). The essential basis of it remained, however, the same: an abhorrence of the class struggle, a feeling that hierarchy was of importance, and a belief in the efficacity of corporate structures to bring the classes together to work for the good of the state, and consequently for the good of themselves and their families.

Anti-Semitism

Racism and anti-Semitism were to play an important enough part, in most areas of fascism, for us to need to look at some of their 'intellectual' forebears. Anti-Semitism was endemic throughout central Europe in the nineteenth and early twentieth centuries. As such, it had no need of theorists; though certain theorists of race did emerge in the course of the nineteenth century. Of these, strangely, the two most important were by no means middle European; they were the Frenchman Arthur de

Gobineau (1816-1882) and the Englishman Houston Stewart Chamberlain (1855-1927). The former, in his *Essay on the Inequality of Human Races*, had produced a theory of world history which made of it the perpetual struggle between the races (Caucasian, Negroid, Mongoloid); the latter was an extreme Germanophile, who produced in his 1899 *Foundations of the Nineteenth Century*, originally published in German (the first Lord Redesdale was his English translator), a theory of racism based on the eternal conflict between Aryan and Semite.

While these two writers were exponents of what we might call the 'racial' strand of anti-Semitism, which was to be so influential in Germany and central Europe, an equally important strain of anti-Semitism had emerged during the nineteenth century, based on the economic power of the Jews and their supposed efforts at 'world domination'. The evils engendered by the industrial revolution, and the plight of the urban proletariat, were laid at the door of the capitalist system, and the directors of that financial system became only too readily identified with the Jews. This strain of anti-Semitism was to be particularly effective, initially, on the Left, though it speedily became a weapon in the armoury of the Right as well. Here, the incursion of alien financiers into national economies, and their domination of those economies, became one of the major planks in the platform. By extension, the myth of a Jewish plot to dominate the world via domination of the financial markets became widespread, considerably predating the document which, just after the First World War, appeared to consecrate it – the *Protocols of the Elders of Zion*, which, though almost immediately discovered to be a forgery, has remained a central text of anti-Semitic propaganda to this day (as its prominence on the Internet and on the book-lists of anti-Semitic organisations illustrates).

When we look at the phenomenon of the 'radical Right' in France at the turn of the century, we can see that this particular form of racism was particularly prominent. Its widespread diffusion in this period was in large part based on the influence of Édouard Drumont (1844-1917). This obscure former civil servant came into immediate prominence in 1886 with the publication of his *La France juive* (Jewish France), a turgid 1,200-page book in two volumes which exhaustively pointed the finger at the Jewish power within French society. This was succeeded by other volumes, including *The Testament of an Anti-Semite* in 1891. Drumont's writing was one of the main forces behind the wave of anti-Semitism which swept France in the last decades of the nineteenth century, culminating in the Dreyfus Affair. A Catholic right-winger, his anti-Semitism was based on a hatred of the capitalist system. While, until now, this hatred of the Jew as capitalist had been more common on the Left, Drumont was one of the first to see this doctrine's efficacity for the French Right, which by the end of the century had appropriated it to its own uses. Like many traditionalists, Drumont felt that the 'old values' of pre-Revolutionary society had, throughout the nineteenth century, been undermined by the power of the materialistic bourgeoisie. In this sense, the old Right had, he believed, more in common with the workers than with the capitalists:

The clearest result of the Revolution has been to make the situation of the humble much harder, and on the contrary to fortify the situation of the great and the rich by delivering them from all moral responsibility. [...] Today, thanks to the Jew, money, to which the Christian world merely attached a secondary importance, assigning to it a purely subordinate role, has become all-powerful. Capitalist power, concentrated in a small number of hands, governs as it pleases the whole economic life of the people, enslaves the workers and feasts on iniquitous profits obtained without any toil. [...] Everything comes from the Jew; everything comes back to the Jew.[3]

Drumont's anti-Semitic newspaper *La Libre Parole* (Free Speech), founded in 1892, had a vast circulation, and was of incalculable effect upon public opinion in France in the 1890s and 1900s. His influence was to extend well beyond his death in 1917, being kept alive by the inter-war Right, including particularly figures such as Bernanos and Maurras.

(b) Activists

Though disparate elements of the 'radical Right' are to be found in a number of European nations before the First World War, the two countries in which it appeared at its fullest, strongest and most effective were France and Italy.

The French 'radical Right': Maurice Barrès

One of the defining characteristics of those political activists in France in the four decades before the First World War who have become known as the 'radical Right', alongside their nationalism and authoritarianism, was a strong emphasis on anti-capitalism. In their case, however, this was based in a far more revolutionary attitude than that taken by the essentially conservative Drumont.

An interesting case-study is Maurice Barrès (1862-1923). His platform, when he stood as a Boulangist[4] in the 1889 election, was based on what he called 'national socialism', his programme calling on the one hand for amelioration of the situation of the workers (right to strike, right to unionise, more equitable taxation, etc.), and on the other for the suppression of the parliamentary regime and the formation of a strong executive. This has sometimes been referred to as Barrès's 'socialist' period; but that term would be wrong. Though Barrès, much later, would still refer to Socialists like Jaurès and Sembat as the 'wine waiters at the bar where I drink my liqueur', his combination of nationalism, authoritarianism and anti-capitalism was essentially un-socialist. In the 1889 election, part of Barrès's package had been 'guarantees for French workers against foreign competition' (always a sure-fire vote-winner for the extreme Right); and he also used anti-Semitism as a weapon to mobilise the workers in his support. The French Left had, in the last decades of the nineteenth century, found anti-Semitism to be a particularly effective weapon; with Barrès, and contemporaries of his such as Maurras, this weapon became appropriated by the anti-capitalist Right.

Barrès continued to hold these eclectic views throughout the 1890s. In 1894-5, for example, he edited a newspaper, *La Cocarde*, whose writers contained people from a very wide political spectrum, even taking in anarchism. Yet this journal was united by a number of things, including patriotism, anti-capitalism and anti-parliamentarism. For Barrès Left and Right, if they were national rather than international, were likely to take the same views upon social problems. Barrès's own ideas, as expressed in this paper, appear to have been becoming more and more affected by the left-wing philosopher Proudhon, who was to lie at the basis of so much right-wing social theory in the next fifty years.

In Barrès's *Cahiers*, or notebooks, we find a very illuminating account of the intellectual basis for his nationalism, and for his racism. Much of it stemmed from the ideas of Jules Soury (whom he much admired), with their mistrust of the intellect. Indeed, in his writings in the 1890s Barrès often echoed Soury almost word for word, pronouncing the inability of human reason to reach truth, and saying that 'a truth is only a truth to the extent that one believes it to be true'. Soury's physiological theories, however, led Barrès much further:

> The individual! His intelligence, his capability of grasping the laws of the universe! We must climb down from this claim. We are not the masters of the thoughts that are born within us. They do not come from our intelligence; they are ways of reacting where ancient physiological dispositions are translated. According to the environment in which we have been plunged, we develop judgements and reasonings. Human reason is so shackled that we all go back over the footsteps of our predecessors. There are no personal ideas.

This appears to be a dead end; but Barrès finds a ray of hope, in the idea of what we would now call 'the collective unconscious':

> In this excessive humiliation, a magnificent sweetness brings us some peace, and invites us to accept all our slaveries, and even death: it is the fact that [...] we are the continuity of our parents.

This led directly to Barrès's doctrine of 'la terre et les morts' (the land and the dead), whereby the essence of the French nation lay in the land on which Frenchmen were born, and their forebears who had lived there. His reasoning led ineluctably to the view that what was important was the nation; and if truth was unobtainable through reason, and truth was different for each group of people, the 'nation's truth' was what was valid for members of a nation:

> What is truth? – It is not knowing things, it is finding a certain point, a single point, that point, no other, from which all things appear to us in true proportion. I need to sit down at the exact place for which my eyes (as they have been created for me by the centuries) call out, that place from which all things arrange themselves on the scale of a Frenchman. The totality of these true and just relationships between given objects and a given man, the Frenchman, that totality is French truth and French justice; finding these relationships, is French reason.'

This reasoning can lead, too, to a justification for anti-Semitism; for, if the 'nation's truth' can only be shared by members of a common background, the Jews must be perceived as alien to that experience. As Barrès wrote:

> What I possess of another blood fortifies me in my repugnance for Protestantism (a secular education different from mine) and Judaïsm (a race opposed to mine). [...] The Jews have no country in the sense that we understand it. For us, our country is our soil and our ancestors, it is the land of our dead. For them, it is the place where they find their greatest advantage.[5]

Barrès shows us, more clearly than any other political writer, the close links between the relativist and anti-rational philosophies of the late nineteenth century and the fervent nationalism, authoritarianism, irrationality and racism of so many of the political movements inspired by them.

The French 'radical Right': Action Française

Not all the radical Right, of course, thought things out as subtly as Barrès; and many placed themselves more unequivocally in the front line of direct action. The Marquis de Morès (1858-1896), for example, before his premature death in 1896, was something of an upper-class thug who indulged in street politics of a particularly violent nature. In 1890 he had founded, in the working-class areas of eastern Paris, a 'Comité de la rue Sainte-Anne', in which middle-class Rightists rubbed shoulders with workers and with anarchists. His policies were strongly anti-capitalist (calling for the workers' rights to unionisation and to proper pension schemes) and anti-Semitic (he was for a time Drumont's chief collaborator in his Anti-Semitic League). His main supporters were on the one hand the Catholic aristocracy, and on the other the lower middle classes and the workers of eastern Paris, and particularly the slaughtermen of the La Villette abattoirs, to whom his anti-Semitism particularly appealed. He founded, based on La Villette, a movement called 'Morès and his friends' (*Morès et ses Amis*), which continued well after his death, calling itself by this time 'The friends of Morès' (*Les Amis de Morès*). This movement was at the centre of most populist right-wing demonstrations and activities in France in the last years of the century. Barrès, Maurras and many others kept Morès's memory alive, seeing him as a pioneer of French national socialism.

The apparent dichotomy between philosophical theories and direct action, on the radical Right, was not however as clear as many would have thought. One of the best examples of this is the long-lived Action Française movement (founded at the height of the Dreyfus Affair in 1899, and lasting till 1945), in which both aspects lived alongside each other. On the one hand its leader, Charles Maurras (1868-1952), and a number of other prominent members, presented it as an intellectual movement, in which ideas predominated. On the other hand there was within the movement a cult of violence. Alongside Maurras's intellectual lessons, in his books and in his regular articles in the daily *L'Action française*, there stood the simple doctrines of hatred promulgated by the violent editorials of his lieutenant Léon Daudet (1867-1942), who called his readers to action against their enemies and against the hated minorities. Maurras and Daudet were sometimes contrasted with each other, as 'the Don Quixote and the Sancho Panza' of the movement. But Maurras did not hesitate to write in the same spirit as Daudet, when the situation demanded it. And in the movement at large, alongside the intellectual meetings of the 'Cercle Proudhon', there were the violent demonstrations in the streets, the brawls which centred on the shock troops of Action Française, the 'Camelots du Roi' ('The King's street pedlars'). When you look at the police archives for as late as the Thirties, you find that, among the many riots that took place involving all the various 'fascist' leagues, the largest number of police were wounded at those conducted by Action Française.

It will be important for us to look closely at Action Française, not only for its important place in what we have called 'pre-fascism', and not only because it was to become a bone of contention among political historians and political scientists as to whether, in the inter-war period, it qualified as 'fascist' or not; but also because, of all the movements extant in this early period, it was the one which continued to predominate in the later, 'fascist' period; and because it exerted so much influence on native movements in other European countries in that later period (including Portugal, Spain, Greece, Belgium and even Wales), and will therefore raise for us all kinds of questions about the 'fascist' or 'non-fascist' natures of those movements as well. It has become the custom, in scholarly circles, to dismiss Action Française from any discussion of fascism. As one scholar has put it: 'The Action Française (which most historians do not consider to have been a fascist movement) [...]'.[6] The amount of space accorded to Action Française throughout this present volume is evidence that, for this writer, such hard-and-fast categorisation is far from the truth.

Shortly after the movement's foundation in 1899, Action Française became dominated by Charles Maurras, under whom the movement soon became Royalist. The new kind of Royalism involved was a far cry, however, from the moribund monarchism of the late nineteenth century.[7] It introduced all kinds of radical policies which completely rejuvenated the doctrine, and made of Action Française one of the most successful mass political movements in French history. These policies were nationalist, corporatist, authoritarian, Catholic, anti-Semitic, anti-masonic, and (at the start) anti-capitalist. The movement shared a number of attributes of the contemporary Left; Charles Maurras's first description of the small group of people who decided to found the movement was: 'The nuance is nationalist, with some propensities to socialism'.[8] The corporatism of the movement stemmed directly from the economic and political theories of the nineteenth century, and above all from the teachings of Le Play, filtered through the modern theorist the Marquis de la Tour du Pin, who himself became closely associated with Action Française. The movement insisted, too, that its ideas stemmed from another great nineteenth-century figure, Pierre Proudhon, whom it acclaimed as 'one of our masters'.

Proudhon (1809-1865) is at first sight an unusual forebear to be chosen by a movement of the Right. Described in the text-books as an 'anarchist and social theorist', his best-known statement in his book *Qu'est-ce que la propriété?* (*What is Property?*) (1840), is 'Property is theft'. But Action Française was attracted by both positive and negative aspects of Proudhon's doctrines: on the positive side, his traditionalism, nationalism, and belief in the family as the main social group; on the negative side, his hatred of the French Revolution, of Republicanism, of democracy, of parliament and parliamentarians, of bourgeois capitalists, and of course of the Jews. They set up a 'Cercle Proudhon', which, in its *Cahiers*, stressed all these ideas.

Action Française stood, then, on the one side for nationalism, tradition, and religion (though Maurras was an agnostic, he believed in the value of religion as a force for order; and the largest support for the movement came from the Catholic public); on the other side, particularly in this pre-war period, it stood for a reorganisation of society on corporate lines, for a defence of the workers against the deleterious effects of the bour-geois capitalist society; and for the use of force to achieve these ends. All this was reinforced by a series of hatreds; hatred of democracy of course, but in particular a hatred of the 'minority groups' within society which appeared to be taking it over, by secretly helping each other to positions of power. Maurras identi-fied what he called four 'States within the State': Jews, freemasons, protestants, and 'métèques'; this last word was an invention of his own, taken from the Greek word for an alien living within the city.

From 1906 onwards Action Française began to take a more active line on social issues. This coincided with what appeared to many to be a potentially revolutionary situation; between 1906 and 1911 there were perpetual strikes. Action Française began forging links with the trade unions, and speaking publicly about the similarity of their aims. During the coal strikes of 1908, which Clemenceau 'the strike-breaker' was to put down so bloodily, with support from politicians of all hues in the Chamber of Deputies, AF placed itself in alliance with the anarcho-syndicalist Confédération Générale du Travail (CGT) on the side of the striking miners. Léon Daudet violently denounced the so-called 'liberals' who were now in power, grinding the workers down. When the leaders of the CGT were arrested by Clemenceau, Maurras castigated those conservatives who had backed this move, and who did not realise the importance of the syndicalist movement. Alongside this, Daudet mocked the 'lefties' who were now terrified of the proletariat; the parliamentary socialists, he claimed, were so embarrassed that they had to call the soldiers who had fired on the miners 'the workers of the barracks'.

Maurras's statements on the social question on the occasion of this strike showed his fundamental belief that the class struggle was inevitable in a democratic society. What was needed, he said, was a complete change of regime, the installation of an authoritarian monarchy, which would show both employers and workers that they had common interests, and that any differences could be resolved by each class being aware of its own duties rather than asserting the duties of others. In his depiction of the present situation, however, he made it clear that class struggle was inevitable, and that the needs of the workers should be understood by the bourgeoisie, rather than ignored. The attitudes of the employers created the reactions of the workers.

So in the present unsatisfactory world, faced by the reality of the class struggle, it was important not to side with the forces of capitalism. The workers, at least, were able to recognise the common enemy, democracy. Between this date and the First World War, Action Française was to undertake various ventures with syndicalists of various hues. Extreme Right and extreme Left appeared to be coming together.

The war was to make a difference to Action Française, which by the Twenties had changed a number of its attitudes and emphases. It was to become, in that period, an interesting contemporary of the new 'fascism'. For the moment, in this prewar incarnation, it is one of the best and most successful examples of that pre-fascist radical Right that we have been examining.

Italy

France has been taken as our main example in the years leading up the First World War, mainly because it contained the most important elements of pre-fascist activity. We must not forget, however, that other countries shared in the same experiences, Italy in particular. The Italian writer Marinetti (1876-1944), the founder of the Futurist movement in 1909, was strongly affected by Nietzsche and Sorel. As Shirley Vinall has written: 'Nietzscheanism, social Darwinism, and Sorel's celebration of the heroic qualities of direct action all lie behind Marinetti's glorification of the beauty of struggle, whether in war or social revolution'.[9] On a more active political level, Giovanni Papini (1881-1956), who on a 1905 visit to Paris had met Sorel, sought for Sorellian 'myths' to enthuse the nation, and found them in the images of Imperial Rome; he aimed for a national renewal which would single out those Nietzschean elements in society that were destined to survive and dominate. He called for a new elite of 'homines novi'. At the same time, Enrico Corradini (1865-1931) denounced democratic government, deplored the weakness of bourgeois society, spoke of health and violence in Sorellian and Nietzschean terms, sought for new economic opportunities for the proletariat, and expressed a visceral anti-capitalism, calling in 1909 for a new 'national syndicalism'.

It was in 1910 that Corradini and others founded the Italian Nationalist Association (ANI), which within a short time developed a policy based on the idea of an authoritarian corporate state. As conflicts between classes were inevitable, both workers and employers needed to be organised, he believed. Like the French radical Right, Corradini and his Sorellian companions allied themselves to syndicalism, 'pinning [their] colours firmly to the mast of syndicalism', and believing that 'the syndicate [trade union] must become the basis of economic life'.[10]

The approach of war was to sharpen all these attitudes, as a wide variety of figures, faced by the original Italian neutrality, came out firmly in support of Italian participation (Italy was to declare war on 23 May 1915). On the more literary front, the Futurist Marinetti saw war as the opportunity for a glorious, dynamic Italian future, and the sweeping from power of all the foes that had been keeping her back: 'diplomats, professors, philosophers, archaeologists, critics, cultural obsession, Greek, Latin, senilism, museums, libraries, the tourist industry'.[11] More politically, Giovanni Papini deplored the weak state to which Italy had been brought by old, incompetent leaders, and hailed war as the opportunity for the new generation to try to raise the nation up again; after such a war, he thought, it would be possible to change the class system, and breed a new class of rulers.

The revolutionary Left took up some of the same themes. In October 1914 revolutionary syndicalists set up the *Fascio di azione internazionale* (League for International Action), with the double aim of promoting intervention in the war, and bringing about economic and social change. The title was soon changed to *Fasci di azione rivoluzionaria* (Leagues for Revolutionary Action). Within a month of the founding of this movement, it was joined by a young revolutionary socialist called Benito Mussolini (1883-1945), who had been strongly influenced, for some time past, by Marx, Nietzsche and Sorel. He himself was to describe his brand of socialism as 'a little Bergson mixed with a lot of Blanqui'.[12] In an inflammatory article entitled 'Courage!' ('Audacia!'), in his newly-founded journal *Il Popolo d'Italia*, Mussolini on 15 November 1914 castigated anti-war propaganda as cowardly, anti-revolutionary, and disastrous to the national and international interests of the proletariat.

The war on which Europe had embarked was to be a catalyst in the fortunes of the 'radical Right', not just in Italy but throughout Europe. We shall see, in its aftermath, new elements being added to this volatile cocktail.

1. Jules Soury, quoted by Maurice Barrès, in *Le Journal*, 24 November 1899.

2. Friedrich Nietzsche, *Der Wille zur Macht* (the Will to Power), Aphorisms 955 and 960. (*Sämtliche Werke*, Alfred Kroner Verlag, Stuttgart, 1964, Band IX). My translation.

3. Édouard Drumont, extracts from *Testament d'un Antisémite* (1891) and *La France juive* (1886).

4. General Boulanger, who had become very popular as War Minister 1886-8, appeared likely to come to power in a Right-wing coup in 1889, which for various reasons failed. He had attempted to appeal to all sections of society, from monarchists to the Left; and, even after his failure, a number of his former supporters continued to advocate radical policies which appealed both to workers and to the Right. In a sense, the Boulangists were the first expression of the French 'radical Right'.

5. Maurice Barrès, *Scènes et doctrines du nationalisme*, Paris 1902.

6. Roger Griffin, *Fascism*, p. 297.

7. See Richard Griffiths, 'From Nostalgia to Pragmatism: French Royalism and the Dreyfus Watershed', in *The Right in France*, ed. Atkin and Tallett, Tauris 1997, pp. 115-28.

8. Letter from Charles Maurras to Maurice Barrès, 3 February 1899, published in: *La République ou le Roi: Correspondance inédite 1888-1923* (Paris, Plon, 1970), p. 207.

9. Shirley Vinall, 'The Contradictions of Marinetti: Right-wing Revolutionary and Francophile Nationalist', in *The Pen and the Sword*, ed. Richard Griffiths, 2000, p. 15.

10. Enrico Corradini, 'Associazione Nazionalista Italiana', in *Il nazionalismo* (ANI, Rome, 1920), quoted in Roger Griffin, *Fascism*, OUP 1995, p. 38.

11. Marinetti, 'Manifesto agli studenti', 29 November 1914, quoted in Griffin, op.cit., p. 26.

12. Auguste Blanqui (1805-1881) was a French revolutionary socialist, who took a prominent part in the revolutions of 1830 and 1848, and in the Commune in 1871. He believed that armed rebellion was the main instrument of political change.

2
Avanti!

The Post-War Scene in Europe, and the Success of Italian Fascism

Some new trends: anti-communism and the cult of the ex-serviceman

The First World War added some new characteristics to the profile of the radical Right. The first of these was the myth of renewal through war. Most of the new movements that arose in the immediate post-war period found much of their popular appeal in the cult of the ex-serviceman. Those who had risked their lives in the maelstrom of modern war, it was believed, returned purer, more virile. They were the youth that would replace the old men, the exploiters of society. 'The brutal and bloody apprenticeship of the trenches' had created a 'new aristocracy' who could renew society.[1]

The individual's sense of personal fulfilment was to be found, it was believed, in action. The German writer and soldier Ernst Jünger (1895-1998) was one of the most prominent exponents of this belief. He had fought on the Western Front in the War, receiving Germany's highest military decoration, the *Pour le mérite*. In his war diary, *In Stahlgewittern* (In Storms of Steel), published in 1920, he praised pure action, and suggested that through war the world would be radically altered. He held the post-war sentimental belief in the 'communion of the trenches' which was shared by those, on both sides, who had gone through the same experiences. Above all, he was convinced of the emergence from the war of a heroic elite who would found a new order. His attitude in the nineteen-twenties was a combination of contempt for democracy and the people, and a conviction that through action and heroism society could be revolutionised.

Jünger's beliefs were just an extreme form of the attitudes of a great many returning warriors throughout Europe. At first, it appears to have been writers above all who expressed this belief in the 'healthiness' of war, which might breathe fresh life into the decadent society that had been left behind. In France, figures such as Henry de Montherlant and Pierre Drieu la Rochelle (both strongly influenced by their reading of Nietzsche), exalted male heroism and the fraternity of war, and contrasted these with the 'feminine' nature of contemporary society. But the 'nostalgia of war' was to have far more concrete results than mere literary romanticism. Most of the post-war movements of the radical Right were strongly based in the cult of the ex-serviceman, and of the 'new generation' forged by war, which was going to reform society.

The other main new characteristic brought by the War was the fear of communism. In the aftermath of the Bolshevik Revolution, and of the abortive communist revolutions of the immediate post-war era, fear of a force that so immediately threatened society changed the complexion of the radical Right, which from now on, while remaining revolutionary in its conception of the future society that must be achieved, nevertheless had a central, negative core of opposition to communism. That opposition in many respects redefined this area of the Right. The old pre-war alliances between radical Right and revolutionary Left were no longer possible. Instead, a new myth emerged: that of the creation of a 'third way' between the opposing forces of capitalism and communism. In the process, the relationships between the new-style 'radical Right' and old-style 'conservatism' became far more complex, particularly in the practical sphere.

As we move into the post-war era, an appreciation of the situation of the revolutionary Right becomes far more complex, as the possibility of its achieving power becomes more pronounced. The pre-war 'radical Right' had on the whole taken the form of a series of protest movements, with little prospect of power; but, from 1922 onwards, with the advent to power of Italian Fascism, this picture was to change. In inter-war Europe we will find many differences between fascist movements in power, and fascist movements when in opposition, with the former often having to compromise on what had appeared to be inflexible ideals when they were in opposition. The realities of power will be seen often to produce a more pragmatic approach. Similarly, even within opposition fascism, we will often need to distinguish between theory and practice.

Some new movements 1918-1922

In a number of countries, immediately after the war, new movements and new forms of government emerged. In Portugal, for example, the Integralist movement, *Integralismo Lusitano*, founded in 1914, had based its doctrines on those of Action Française (the very title 'Integralist' echoing Maurras's doctrine of 'nationalisme intégral'). It was in 1918 that the short-lived Sidónio Pais dictatorship came to power in Portugal, establishing in its constitution, under Integralist influence, corporatist representation. But the most dramatic expressions of the new Right were to be found in Germany and Italy.

The chaos and violence of immediate post-war Germany were a fertile breeding-ground for extremist groups of all kinds. The communist threat, close on the heels of the Russian Revolution, was ever-present; there were between 1919 and 1921 attempted communist coups in Berlin, Munich, the Ruhr, Thuringia and Central Germany. The weak republican government had to rely, for defence against such uprisings, on the *Freikorps*, auxiliary armed forces consisting mainly of ex-servicemen, whose political attitudes were mainly nationalistic and anti-democratic. These ex-servicemen shared with many in the population the view that the politicians of the Republic were responsible for Germany's defeat. In 1920 an attempted right-wing *putsch* led by a nationalist called Kapp, and based on the *Freikorps*, showed the dangers to the new Republic from the Right as well as the Left. On both political extremes there was little patience with democratic structures.

Amid all this, there were a number of movements that represented the strain of Right-wing activity that we have been calling 'radical Right', though they had a particularly German tinge to them. Alongside the counter-revolutionary anger of the returning soldiers and much of the civilian population, there was a strong influence of 'völkisch' elements, and much anti-Semitism. (The word 'völkisch' denotes those extreme right-wing elements whose politics were based on racial criteria, and on a vague conception of a 'German' past). Among the new movements of this kind were the *Deutsch-Sozialistische Partei* (German Socialist Party), of which the anti-Semite Julius Streicher (later to be a leading figure in the Nazi party), was a prominent member, and also the *Völkische Werkgemeinschaft* ('Völkisch' Work-Association), headed by Dr Otto Dickel. Amid them, an initially obscure Munich-based movement called the *Deutsche Arbeiterpartei* (German Workers' Party), a nationalist movement which relied heavily on working-class support, emerged amid the turmoil of 1918-23. Soon, this party was to be renamed the *Nazional-Sozialistische Deutsche Arbeiterpartei* (National Socialist German Workers' Party), otherwise known as the NSDAP, or the Nazis for short; and it came under the direction of Adolf Hitler (1889-1945). It became one of the major components of the Bavarian extreme Right, though it had branches in many other parts of Germany. Following the example of the other extreme nationalist movements in Bavaria at this time, the party formed a para-military organisation, the SA, or Brownshirts. And like the other parties, it had as a major part of its platform a virulent anti-Semitism (a constant among extreme movements of Left and Right in Central Europe).

In Italy, the immediate aftermath of the War had brought new figures to the forefront. Gabriele d'Annunzio (1863-1938), the Nietzschean writer who, up to the war, had played merely a peripheral part in active politics, now emerged as a war hero, and a fervent nationalist who was looked to by many as a future leader. In 1919 he led a group of irregular troops to seize, on behalf of Italy, Fiume, the Adriatic city (with an Italian majority among its citizens) which had been given to the new state of Yugoslavia under the peace treaties. He remained in command of Fiume for over a year.

What is interesting, from our viewpoint, is the form of government he set up there. The city's constitution, the Carnaro Charter, was a blend of corporatism and nationalism, containing detailed plans for a State corporative system. Even more significantly, d'Annunzio set about creating nationalist 'myths', with elaborate ceremonies, which linked his 'legionaries' to ancient Rome. He also introduced the 'Roman salute' and the black shirts that were later to be used by Mussolini's Fascists.

Meanwhile, Corradini's pre-war Italian Nationalist Association continued to flourish, with its powerful blend of nationalism and right-wing syndicalism. And Benito Mussolini was emerging as one of the most prominent figures on the radical Right. On 23 March 1919, in Milan, he had founded the *Fasci di combattimento* (Groups for the war veteran). The programme of the *Fasci* was a mixture of Left and Right, and included populist policies such as seizure of church property, abolition of the monarchy, abolition of the Senate, taxes on war profiteers, together with more positive policies such as nationalisation, worker participation, an eight-hour working day, a minimum wage, etc. An outward sign of the new-style nationalism that marked the movement was the adoption of the symbol (which played upon the word *fascio*, or 'group'), of the *fasces*, the axe bound in a bundle of rods, that had been carried by the lictors in Ancient Rome. It symbolised the strength brought about by unity (because each rod could be broken individually, but the bundle could not); but it also provided the link with the heroic Italian past which was later to be so important to Mussolini, and which d'Annunzio in this same year of 1919 was to use to such effect in Fiume.

From now on the members of this movement became known as 'Fascists'; and before long they adopted the black shirt which had been worn by d'Annunzio's followers, many of whom joined the new movement. They also began to use the 'Roman' salute that had been pioneered by d'Annunzio. The organisation was paramilitary.

The early failures of the Nazi party

It is interesting to speculate what the 'radical Right' in Europe in the inter-war period would have been called, and what generic characteristics would have been ascribed to it, if Hitler's Munich putsch of 1923 had succeeded, and if Mussolini's 1922 March on Rome had failed. The myth of 'international fascism' might well have taken a completely different form. But it is no use speculating about such things. The fact is that Mussolini's Fascists were clearly ready for power, and capable of taking it, and that, in the early nineteen-twenties, Hitler's Nazis had nothing like the following, or the capability, of their Italian counterparts.

1923 was a year of crisis for the Weimar Republic. The value of the Reichsmark continually fell, in galloping inflation, until the dollar was equivalent to 130 billion Reichsmarks. The army, and nationalists in general, had been angered by the government's decision not to continue the passive resistance to the French occupation of the Ruhr. Amid continuing unrest, a number of German States, Bavaria included, were considering the possibility of secession. By late 1923 Hitler, in association with the other Bavarian elements of the extreme Right, was planning a concerted right-wing coup, or 'putsch', in Munich. The army and the Bavarian authorities were expected to co-operate in this rebellion, which would then spread to the rest of Germany, and destroy the Republic. The sign for the putsch to start was expected to come from the authorities themselves in early November. However, in the event, Ritter von Kahr, head of the Bavarian government, announced to the conspirators on 6 November that the putsch would not be taking place. Hitler decided, as head of the 'Kampfbund' (the association of Right-wing groups, including the NSDAP, which had been planning the coup) to go ahead regardless. On the 8th he proclaimed a 'national revolution' in the Bürgerbräukeller, one of Munich's main beer-cellars. What the conspirators did not know was that the Head of the Reichswehr (supposedly favourable to the Right-wing cause) had from Berlin, for fear of national chaos, ordered the army to resist the rising. On the 9th, military and police were deployed in the streets of Munich. Though Hitler was indecisive, Field-Marshal von Ludendorff, the hero of the First World War, a strong supporter of the coup, persuaded him to go ahead with the intended march through the city to the Feldherrnhalle, a monument to Bavaria's greatest soldiers. Ludendorff clearly believed that the soldiers would not fire on him, their former Commander-in-Chief; but he was mistaken. The hail of fire that greeted the procession killed sixteen, and wounded many others. In the aftermath, Hitler was put on trial for treason. He received a sentence of five years.

The failure of the Munich putsch set back the cause of the NSDAP. It was not until the late Twenties that it was to come to the forefront of German politics again, this time in a far more dangerous way. The Twenties was, on the other hand, to be the decade of Italian Fascism. The torch of the radical Right had been taken by the Fascists, as from 1922 onwards they consolidated their power in Italy.

Italian Fascism comes to power

In the immediate post-war period Italy experienced an economic and social crisis of daunting proportions, with inflation and unemployment leading to strikes and violence in the years 1919-20, amid fears of a Bolshevik revolution. The Fascist movement began expanding at a rapid rate, and at the same time Mussolini's policies took a sharp turn to the Right. For the next two years the Fascist squads were to exercise considerable violence against their opponents on the Left, whether terrorising individuals, or having larger-scale set battles with their opponents.

Mussolini now began the first of the expedient shifts of position which were to mark the rest of his political career. Fascism had been set up in opposition to the parliamentary system of alliances and compromises; but in 1921 Mussolini negotiated an electoral alliance with the current Prime Minister, the liberal Giolitti. Through this alliance the Fascists won 35 seats in the election of May 1921.

By 1922 Fascist membership had reached about a quarter of a million. Meanwhile, social unrest was continuing, with the Government wavering in face of it. In August, the Left called for a general strike, which looked like paralysing the country. The Fascists issued an ultimatum calling on the Government to prove within 48 hours that it could exert authority, failing which 'Fascism will assume full freedom to supplant the State'. Though the strike soon collapsed, civil unrest continued, with the Fascists destroying communist power-bases, to the approval of a great section of the population that perceived them as doing what the legal government was failing to do.

Meanwhile, in September, Mussolini produced another expedient *volte-face*, by giving up his opposition to the monarchy; and he was already giving out the message that he believed that Fascism should become a more conventional political party. This was at a stage when the current government appeared to be falling apart, and to some Fascists it looked as though their movement could gain power by legitimate means. But other

Fascists believed that their programme could never be carried out by normal parliamentary procedures. On 24 October, after a speech by Mussolini in Naples, the 'March on Rome' was organised. The Fascists arranged to occupy the main public buildings in various Italian cities, and at the same to have a March on Rome by three different routes. On 27 October the plan was carried out. The King, Vittorio Emmanuele II, did not call on the Army, for fear of civil war. On 28 October he offered Mussolini the Prime Ministership, and on the 30th the Fascist troops entered Rome peaceably.

Mussolini included only four Fascists in his Cabinet, out of fourteen members. But he immediately set about providing opportunities for greater powers, including a new electoral law which gave a large number of seats to any party gaining more than 25% of the votes in an election. In elections held in April 1924 under this system, an electoral list centred on the Fascists obtained 275 seats. Fascism now appeared entrenched in power; though it was still functioning within a democratic parliamentary system. In late 1924, however, Mussolini's opportunity came.

The murder of the socialist Giacomo Matteotti by Fascist thugs momentarily seemed to put Mussolini's government's future in jeopardy. But he turned the apparent crisis to advantage. In a speech to the parliament on 3 January 1925 he turned the tables on his opponents by assuming responsibility for all that had happened, and suggested that the only way for Italy to reach calm and stability was for a dictatorship to be instituted. This speech was acclaimed. Many believed that only Mussolini could provide firm government, and feared that if he were to go, the nation would decline into worse violence and chaos than anything that had been seen. In these circumstances Mussolini came to absolute power.

Fascism, in power, became 'respectable'. Its rhetoric now stressed the importance of order and stability, under an authoritarian state, and thereby attracted many conventional conservatives and liberals who had been all too aware of the shortcomings of the previous, often chaotic, democratic regime. Mussolini appeared to be offering a 'new start' for the Italian nation. At the same time much of the radical nature of Fascism in opposition was lost, and the State became the defender of the capitalism on which its prosperity depended. Theorists of Fascism continued to propound the old doctrines, but all that remained of them in practice was the commitment to the Corporate State, towards which the regime worked in the late Twenties, producing by the early Thirties corporate structures throughout the nation's activities. The concept of all economic and social activity being subordinated to the State was now, however, devoted to the defence of capitalism rather than to its replacement. The all-powerful State was to be judged on its achievements; and, as the regime progressed, those achievements were more and more seen in practical terms: the solving of unemployment; the achievements of the new road system; the fact that 'the trains ran on time'; the impression given to the world that, for the first time, a united Italy actually *worked*, and that Italy had achieved thereby a new status.

A significant pointer to the new image that Fascism wished to project was the regime's attitude to the Catholic Church. Mussolini's anti-clericalism was abandoned. Realising the need for traditional Catholic support, he worked closely with the Vatican in the late Twenties. This culminated in the Lateran Treaties of 1929, in which the relationship between church and state was formalised, and the Vatican was declared a sovereign and independent state. Thus was resolved the running sore which had existed ever since the Papal States had been occupied at the time of Italian unification in the late nineteenth century.

Fascism had considerable support from intellectuals, the foremost among them being Giovanni Gentile (1875-1944), who developed a persuasive philosophy of the one-party State. For him, the 'individual', the 'people', the 'Party', the 'Nation' and the 'State' all partook of the same nature, and could take each other's place in the right circumstances. The State was at one and the same time the 'very personality of the individual' and the 'will of the nation'. The Party ceased to be '*a* party', and 'as an organisation of the great majority of the nation or of the politically significant masses of the Italian people becomes *the* Nation'. So it was that individual and collective interests were one and the same.[2]

This accorded with Mussolini's main continuing policy throughout his career, amid all his other changes – that of the authoritarian State, which he described as 'the single, unitary state, the sole repository of the history, of the entire future, of all the force of the Italian nation; [...] a moral idea which incarnates itself and expresses itself in a system of hierarchies; [...] a single national discipline binding upon sect, faction and party.'[3]

In support of the idea of the authoritarian state, Sorellian 'myths' were developed, concentrating on the theme of national continuity, and the restoration of former grandeur. Ancient Rome was evoked not just through the *fasces*, but through the mass meetings, the Roman salutes, the insignia of the legions. In the Thirties, with Mussolini's eyes turning to foreign conquest, these images became even stronger, with the Mediterranean seen as *Mare Nostrum*.

Italian Fascism, both before it came to power and in its early years in government, differed from one of the stereotypes most often associated with 'fascism' nowadays. Just as there was little anti-Semitism in Italy, there was equally little anti-Semitism in the movement, which benefited from Jewish funders in its early days, and which was joined by a higher percentage of the small Italian Jewish population than of the Gentile population. It was only by the late Thirties, under the influence of Hitler's Germany, that anti-Semitism was to play any important part in Mussolini's policies.

As Stuart Woolf has put it, 'The two most fundamental and consistent characteristics of Italian fascism were its nature as a mass party, and the employment of its power in the interests of both social and economic conservation, in the interests of bourgeois capitalism.'[4] Despite the original aims of the movement, and despite the continued writings of a number of Fascist intellectuals and theorists, this was the stark reality of Fascism in power. Only years later, in the Salò Republic set up under the aegis of the Germans in Northern Italy, after Mussolini had been deposed and Italy had made peace with the Allies, was Mussolini's vision of Fascism to return to its radical roots.

1. See Mussolini, 'Trincerocrazia', *Il Popolo d'Italia*, 15 December 1917. Reprinted in Griffin, op.cit., p. 29.

2. Gentile, quoted and paraphrased in A. James Gregor, *The Ideology of Fascism: The Rationale of Totalitarianism*, Collier-Macmillan Ltd., London, 1969, p. 221.

3. Mussolini, 'L'instaurazione dello stato fascista', 1923, quoted in Gregor, op.cit., p. 172.

4. S.J. Woolf, 'Italy', in *European Fascism*, ed. S.J. Woolf, Weidenfeld & Nicolson 1968, p. 45.

3

'The Most Constructive Statesman of this Age, Benito Mussolini'

The Initial Impact of Italian Fascism

We are so used, from our later vantage-point, to seeing 'international fascism' as one of the major features of the inter-war period, that it is hard to realise that this was essentially a phenomenon of the Thirties. In the Twenties, on the contrary, the situation was far less clear. The Italian Fascist regime was a completely new phenomenon, and difficult at first for people from other nations to assess. The Foreign Services of the various European Governments appear to have adjusted to it fairly rapidly; but movements of the Right, within other countries, had a wide range of reactions, and the meaning of the word 'fascist', and its use, tended to vary wildly from movement to movement, and from country to country. There was little sense of an 'international movement' being formed on the Italian base; and the Italians themselves do not seem to have been looking for one. Though Mussolini aimed to 'export' Fascism to all Italian expatriates, he does not at this stage seem to have seen it as 'exportable' in any other way. It was not until the early Thirties that this was to become one of his concerns.

The picture, in the nineteen-twenties, is therefore an extremely fragmented one. It will be worth our taking various examples of the interpretations placed upon the word 'Fascism' in this period, and of the way in which movements of the Right interwove these concepts with their own concerns.

General public reactions

The accolades which had been so enthusiastically and gratuitously cast upon him by conservative writers and public figures in the nineteen-twenties and early thirties had been so frequent and so unequivocally phrased that he had no trouble in believing that he was indeed the greatest statesman of his time.[1]

So Christopher Hibbert has written of Mussolini. And there is no doubt that, in a decade when statesmanship, after the rejection of Lloyd George in Britain and Clemenceau in France, had seemed almost non-existent, Mussolini appeared to stand head and shoulders above the politicians of Europe. Italy, as the Twenties unrolled, began to present, to many, the picture of a country that had turned from chaos to order, from widespread poverty to comparative affluence. Many were impressed by the rhetoric of Fascism, which made Italy once more seem a great nation, worthy to be consulted on international issues. To the inhabitants of countries that appeared to be losing their pride and their imperial past, this regeneration of 'Italian self-respect' seemed one of the most important features of the regime. Almost equally important, in the feverish post-war obsession with the dangers of communism, was Fascism's successful stand against the forces of that doctrine.

One must realise, however, that for many outside observers it was nevertheless seen as a purely Italian phenomenon. British reactions were typical in this respect, particularly in Foreign Office circles, where, as in the F.O.'s later reactions to Salazar's regime in Portugal, it appears to have been felt that 'Mediterranean types' needed the smack of firm government. The Foreign Secretary Austen Chamberlain, for example, thought Mussolini to be a wonderful man, because he was 'working for the greatness of his country', but believed that there was 'no greater mistake than to apply British standards to un-British conditions. Mussolini would not be a Fascist if he were an Englishman in England'.[2] Winston Churchill, on a visit to Italy in 1927, stated his views as follows:

If I had been an Italian, I am sure that I should have been wholeheartedly with you from start to finish in your triumphant struggle against the bestial appetites and passions of Leninism. [...] But in England we have not had to fight this danger in the same deadly form. We have our way of doing things.[3]

It is hindsight which makes this general benevolence towards Fascism, among the nations of Western Europe, of any great importance in itself, as at the time the Italian regime must have seemed almost irrelevant to their major concerns. The Italian experiment was admired, but from a distance; and it hit the head-lines only when specific events forced themselves on the attention of the world. The occupation of Corfu and the murder of Matteotti were two such events, in the early years of Fascism; but once the ripples of these had died down, Fascism became almost taken for granted, as a highly successful political experi-ment, and a permanent part of the European scene.

That, then, was the general reaction in the areas of political power in the other European nations. Fascism was taken on its record as a form of government, rather than on its doctrines and supposed aims (most of which had already been abandoned or recycled in different forms). The press of Centre and Right, in France and Britain, was almost unanimous in its praise of the 'return to calm and order' in Italy, which was ascribed entirely to the Fascist party. An article in the ultra-respectable *Revue des deux mondes*, on 15 December 1922, shows just how far Mussolini had succeeded in calming moderate foreign opinion:

> Violence passes and laws remain. The first acts of M. Mussolini are reassuring and indicate a sound under-standing of the necessities of the moment, and the aspirations of the country. [...] This movement has nothing reactionary in it, in the sense that the political parties give to that word, but it is conservative in the true meaning of that fine word which expresses the people's first and most permanent need, that for stability and order.

There were, of course, a number of political scientists and commentators who were bowled over by the 'ideas' of fascism; some of them even set up an international study body, the CINEF (International Centre for Fascist Studies), based in Lausanne. The scholars involved were, however, mostly specialists on Italy (such as Professor Walter Starkie of Dublin and Professor Edmund Gardner of London), even if their pronouncements betrayed an excess of enthusiasm for the new experiment; and most of the other members of CINEF tended to have Italian connections.

In other circles, however, Fascism was, for a few years after its appearance, to have a practical influence; though that influence seems to have taken many different forms, according to people's varying understanding of the Italian movement's political philosophy and activities.

Some early uses of the name 'Fascism', in England and France

Understanding of what Italian Fascism stood for was at best muddled, in the Western parliamentary democracies. Given the discrepancy we have seen between Fascism's aims when in opposition, and its characteristics when in power, this is hardly surprising. The one thing on which all observers were agreed, however, was Fascism's role as a bulwark against communism.

The use of the actual word 'Fascism' is something of a special case at this stage. France, and Britain, appear to have been the two main countries where the word was used to describe newly-formed indigenous movements (which were often insignificant in membership or influence). Three examples of this stand out, for the completely different nature of the ideas and activities of the movements concerned. One, in France, was a radical, anti-capitalist movement which had much in common with what Italian Fascism had stood for before it came into power; and, of the two English examples, one was a group of old-fashioned Conservatives obsessed by the threat of revolution, and determined on the maintenance of the *status quo*, the other a virulently anti-Semitic group, whose concentration on that theme above all others showed it to be completely out of phase with the Italian movement.

Probably the earliest European movement, outside Italy, to use the name 'Fascist' was an extraordinary group formed in England as early as 1923. This was the 'British Fascisti', known from 1924 as the 'British Fascists, Ltd' (and called by their opponents the 'BFs'). They were basically a Conservative movement, obsessed with the dangers of civil emergency. In these years the emergence of the Labour Party as a formidable political power, coupled with the publicity about trades union policies of

achieving political objectives by direct industrial action, reinforced the fears, in the traditional Right, that had been
engendered by the Russian Revolution. As a result, military and
patriotic people such as these felt the need to create organisations consisting of 'disinterested patriots [...] ready to serve their
country in any adversity',[4] which could counter this threat, maintain public order, and guarantee essential services.

Membership of the movement appears to have been mainly
military, naval and 'county', and, though the lower ranks
contained loyal working-class toughs, the Grand Council
contained mainly peers, generals and admirals. On the enrol-
ment form, entrants undertook 'to uphold His Most Gracious
Majesty King George V, his heirs and successors, the established
constitution of Great Britain, and the British Empire', and to
'render every service in my power to the British Fascisti in their
struggle against all treacherous and revolutionary movements
now working for the destruction of the Throne and Empire'.
Union Jacks were the main insignia, and the movement's motto
was 'For King and Country'. Among the movement's activities
was the stewarding of Conservative Party meetings. As an
admirer of Italian Fascism remarked with disgust: 'There was no
Fascism, as I understood it, in the organisation, which was
merely Conservatism With Knobs On; it was justified by the Red
attempts to smash up meetings of the Right, but it should never
have been misnamed.'[5]

Another movement to use the name 'Fascist' in Britain in the
Twenties was the Imperial Fascist league, founded in 1929 by
Arnold Leese (1878-1956). This movement represents yet
another strand in the complex web of uses made of this name.
Here, though Leese made obeisance towards corporatist ideas,
the movement was above all concerned with matters which
played little part in the policies of Italian Fascism: the most
important of these was anti-Semitism.

Leese was a veterinary surgeon specialising in the diseases of
camels, who, after his retirement to Lincolnshire, came under
the influence of Arthur Kitson, the monetary reformer, who was
a member of The Britons, a violently anti-Semitic group that had
been set up in 1919. Like most of the early twentieth-century
monetary reformers, Kitson believed that the Jews were at the
basis of all the ills of the present monetary system, and that their

aim was world domination through 'debt-slavery'. Leese later described how Kitson had introduced him to 'the Jewish Menace', lending him a copy of the *Protocols of the Elders of Zion*, in which Leese found everything to 'ring true'.

In the same year that he met Kitson, Leese became interested in Italian Fascism; this interest was apparently kindled at first for completely different reasons. 'I had watched', he wrote, 'the bloodless revolution of Mussolini, who by sheer determination had ended the chaos into which Liberalism (disguised) had brought his country; it appeared to me that here was a movement which might end political humbug.'[6]

The Imperial Fascist League started by producing a certain amount of theory compatible with the Italian model: an Upper House appointed by the state, consisting of eminent members of the community, and a Lower House to which representatives of industry and other national occupations would be appointed; the executive being a Grand Council. But these ideas blended ill with another of Leese's major concerns: the reduction of governmental interference in almost every sphere of life. And these ideas, contradictory as they were, were to play very little part in the publicity and the activities of the movement, which were predominantly concerned with the Jewish threat. The Imperial Fascist League was to last throughout the Thirties, being, after the advent of Nazism to power, far more in accord with that movement than with Italian Fascism. Sir Oswald Mosley was to describe it as 'one of those crank little movements [...] mad about the Jews.' Leese was to respond by calling Mosley's British Union of Fascists 'Kosher Fascism', because he thought Mosley was soft on the Jews.

Neither of these two British movements had any political importance. The Imperial Fascist League, in particular, was a fringe group of small membership. They have both shown us, nevertheless, how the 'Fascist' concept could be taken over by people whose preoccupations were very different from those of Mussolini's movement. They have also made clear the variety of interpretations that could be placed upon the word 'Fascism' in this period.

In France, on the other hand, Georges Valois's *Le Faisceau* (the bundle, or 'fasces', founded in 1925), which used the name of Fascism (though allusively), in its title, was a very different matter. Unlike the British experiments, this movement's founder knew exactly what he understood by 'Fascism', and was very much in tune with many of the original aims the Italian movement had pursued before its access to power, aims which he saw as being very much in the French pre-war tradition, of which he had been a part.

Valois (1878-1945) had been a prominent member of the pre-war Action Française, and had been heavily involved in the anti-capitalist activities of that movement. In his powerful articles for the fortnightly *Revue de l'Action Française*, and in his 1908 book *Social Revolution or the King*, he had called for rights of association for the workers, and the use of economic growth to aid the masses. He helped to found the Cercle Proudhon, and played a leading part in the collaboration with the anarcho-syndicalists which had been so remarkable a feature of the pre-war Action Française.

In the post-war period, a number of members of Action Française began to see the movement as moving too strongly towards being the defender of the interests of the bourgeoisie against revolutionary socialism and communism. For a while, however, the old radical ideas continued to be promulgated within the movement by people such as Valois, with Maurras's approval.

It appears to have been a growing exasperation with Maurras's methods, rather than with the social ideas now being espoused by important sections of the movement, that led to Valois breaking with Action Française. He felt that the revolutionary fervour had gone out of the movement: 'My firm aim had been to drag the whole Action Française into a revolutionary movement. I held it to be governed by men who were perfectly determined not to act.'[7] The example of Mussolini, with whom he had been impressed on a visit to Italy in 1923, and with whose ideas his own seemed so much in tune, stood before him; and the advent of the Cartel des Gauches, a left-wing coalition, into government in 1924, proved a further spur. Valois set up, in 1925, his own movement, 'Le Faisceau'.

The movement's most public face was that of its paramilitary units, dressed in blue shirts. Its aim was to replace the Republic with a dictatorship, and to destroy party politics.

Though he used a name that was clearly based on that of the

Italian movement, and paraded his shock troops on the Italian model, Valois stressed the essentially *French* nature of his movement, claiming that it was based above all on the lessons of Barrès and Sorel. The French tradition of the 'radical Right' can thus be seen to have haunted its successors in the inter-war period, to the extent that 'the influence of Fascism' could at times merely have seemed to be the addition to the old policies of a name and of a 'fashionable' contemporary allusion that could draw attention to a foreign experiment which had succeeded (unlike the French home-grown radical Right) in scaling the heights of power.

Valois was, because of the Italians' success, determined to publicise, particularly in Italy itself, the correlation between his movement and Mussolini's. He wrote a book called *French Fascism*, which appeared in Italian in 1926. In it, he stressed the fact that since the War the state had an all-important economic function, which was hampered by the warring forces within society. The only solution was to impose discipline, by the creation of a 'unitary or fascist state existing above parties and classes'. This state, by basing itself on war veterans, workers and peasants, could harness the dangerous modern economic forces, to provide a system based on social justice. This was, Valois claimed, what 'social Catholics, socialists and communists' had been seeking for fifty years. If everyone could raise themselves above their 'old class habits', they could find the solution in 'the national State'.[8]

Though this seems so redolent of Italian Fascism, it was in fact a recycling of Action Française ideas from the Cercle Proudhon, in which the model of Le Play's and La Tour du Pin's corporatism was seen as the solution to the social and economic ills that so concerned both the Left and the radical Right in this period; while the need for an all-powerful State headed by a dictator-figure was also part of the pre-war concerns of people such as Barrès. Valois was thus making use of Italy's success to validate previously-held opinions.

Le Faisceau, at its height, reached about 60,000 members. It at first appeared to be outstripping its main rivals, Action Française and a new movement, the Jeunesses Patriotes, which had been founded in 1924 and about which more later. By 1927, however, Le Faisceau was dying, mainly because of lack of funds.

Le Faisceau, for a short period, had had more claim to influence and power than the two British examples we have seen. But it would be wrong to think of it as having been in any way politically important. The Thirties fascist writer Robert Brasillach (1909-1945), looking back on the Twenties in his autobiography *Notre Avant-guerre*, deplored the fact that Italian Fascism had received so little echo in French politics in that period:

> The only thing that Italian Fascism had given rise to in France was a pale imitation, led by a highly questionable lunatic called Georges Valois, a movement which we laughed to scorn, but which was joined, I later learned, by a number of honest dupes [...] We could find nothing that represented, better than Action Française, the aspirations of nationalist youth, a kind of 'pre-fascism' which was already in the air.[9]

Le Faisceau is nevertheless important for the glimpse it gives us of the relationship that could exist between the new Italian movement and existent trends in the radical Right. There were, in France and elsewhere in the Twenties (as in Germany), other movements of the 'radical Right', which did not advertise any connection with Italian Fascism either in their title or in their propaganda; it will be worth our now assessing *their* relationships with the new movement.

Other movements of the radical Right in the Twenties

We have already seen the prominent role played by the radical Right in post-war Germany. In France, the most prominent pre-war movement of this type, Action Française, continued in existence after the War, though its nature and influence changed considerably; and alongside it a new movement, the Jeunesses Patriotes, came into prominence.

The War had changed the situation of Action Française, and in some respects changed its character. In the interests of national unity, the movement had suspended its attacks on the regime at the outbreak of war. By its patriotic propaganda it came to be seen as something of a national institution. In 1917, it had consolidated its position within France by its prominent role in publicising the spy scare which, by falsely implicating ministers and ex-ministers, led to the fall of the government. By allying itself with Clemenceau, who thereby came into power with quasi-dictatorial powers in order to pursue the war effort, Action Française had not only shown its powers over public opinion, but had also appeared to forge a place for itself in the corridors of power. The movement emerged from the War, then, with a new respectability, and as a kind of national symbol. This gave it such confidence that, in the 1919 elections, it for the first time put up parliamentary candidates – though, because Action Française over-confidently refused to make any electoral pacts with the rest of the Right, the 'Bloc National', only four of these candidates got in.

The new 'respectability' of Action Française was matched by a change of attitude in relation to social matters, where the old radicalism was, in certain quarters of the movement, sidelined. Volumes and articles expatiating on the virtues of the bourgeoisie as the backbone of France were produced. Despite this, the old anti-capitalist rhetoric still remained a part of the movement's general stock-in-trade.

The immediate post-war years marked the height of Action Française's power and influence. The Catholic church seemed to have taken it to its heart, to the extent that it has been described as wielding a 'dictatorship' over Catholic intellectual circles. The failure of its parliamentary efforts could be seen as having been merely the result of adopting a false tactic; the movement returned to its extra-parliamentary roots. The daily newspaper *L'Action Française* had a vast circulation. All seemed to be going well: but the seeds of decline were there. Firstly, there came Valois's decision to break away, in 1925. He took with him many members, and also attracted away a number of important financial supporters. Another new movement, the 'Jeunesses Patriotes', founded in 1924, was also attracting many people from the older movement's constituency. And then, in 1926, there came a bolt from the blue; the Papal condemnation of the Action Française movement, which meant that every Catholic who read the newspaper was excommunicated, and deprived of the sacraments.

The resultant crises of conscience did lead a number of Catholics to prefer their Action Française principles to the sacraments, it is true; but the condemnation nevertheless was one of the contributory factors to the comparative decline of the movement in the late Twenties. Later, in the Thirties, it was to give the appearance, on the public stage, of losing out to the other 'fascist' leagues of that period. But one must never underestimate the impact that Action Française had had, and continued to have, on the ideas of whole generations of Frenchmen, many of them prominent in their respective fields. Action Française was still strong enough in these quarters to be a major influence upon the policies of Marshal Pétain's Vichy government in 1940.

What relationship, if any, was there between Action Française and Mussolini's Fascism in the Twenties? Many observers noted the similarities between the two movements. Léon Daudet responded angrily to suggestions that Fascism had influenced the French movement: 'We imitate nobody', he said in *L'Action Française* of 29 January 1923; 'we are not the result of any other movement, least of all contemporary Italian Fascism.' Many French commentators suggested that it was Action Française's doctrines that had, in fact, inspired those of Italian Fascism. And there is no doubt that the two movements had a great deal in common, not just in their shared enemies, but also in many of their positive doctrines. Though Maurras perceived certain differences, such as the Fascist concentration on the State, he saw lessons for France in Fascism's methods, and he was pleased to think of Mussolini as some kind of apt pupil. Léon Daudet, by 1926, saw a 'Latin' alliance with Catholic Italy as being the best way to combat both Germany and international freemasonry. That there were major differences between the two movements is not in doubt; but if contemporary perceptions were anything to go by, many in the AF saw Italian Fascism as being some kind of offshoot of their policies (much as Portuguese Integralism actually was).

The Jeunesses Patriotes represent yet another strand of the French extra-parliamentary Right. The movement's founder, Pierre Taittinger (of the famous champagne firm) (1887-1967), was a prosperous businessman who, pre-war, had been a follower of the ideas of Maurice Barrès, and a member of one of the radical Right groups of that period, the Ligue des Patriotes. He had also been a Bonapartist; and his political ideas, on the importance of creating a strong executive and curbing the powers of 'corrupt' democratic politicians, owed much both to Barrès and to

Bonapartism. In 1924 Taittinger formed the Jeunesses Patriotes, originally seen as a youth wing of the old Ligue des Patriotes (though by 1926 it had broken away from the older, more moribund movement – or rather, the older movement had been deterred by the violence and extremism of its offspring). The JP was a paramilitary movement, and strongly based in the cult of the ex-serviceman; though, as its main platform was anti-communism, Taittinger continually stressed the 'defensive' nature of his shock troops. The title 'Jeunesses' could be misleading, as many members were middle-aged or even elderly; in 1934 the eighty-year-old Marshal Lyautey was proudly to proclaim 'Je suis JP' ('I am a 'Patriotic Youth')!

Despite a certain amount of left-wing anti-capitalist rhetoric, the movement's main aim was the maintenance of middle-class prosperity. Taittinger's publicly declared views on taxation make this clear:

> Commerce and industry are the sources of national energy, the basis of public prosperity. We should encourage them instead of pressuring them. Let us unify the innumerable taxes that harass producers. [...] The inheritance tax as it is presently applied discourages saving, stops the rise of the middle classes [...] An inheritance is not a gift that falls on you from the sky, it is a deposit that your parents bequeath to you to transmit, increased, to your descendants. It is the floating capital of a family across the centuries. It does not belong to the State. It must be sacred.[10]

Though the bases of JP thought would seem to be an amalgam of Bonapartism and of that conservative reaction to the communist threat that we have found in the British Fascisti, the movement, like so many European conservatives, showed admiration for Mussolini and his achievements, above all because of the strength with which he had addressed himself to the problems of his nation. Like so many others in their period, they seem to have seen in Italian Fascism what they wished to see (in other words, whatever was in accordance with their own attitudes), and to have ignored or been ignorant of anything that was not.

All the French extra-parliamentary Right found itself, however, by the late Twenties, in a very much weaker position, compounded by the decline of Le Faisceau after 1927, coupled with Action Française's problems after the papal condemnation of 1926. The Jeunesses Patriotes did not escape the general decline. It was to take the crisis of the early Thirties for such movements as the JP and AF to come once more into prominence on the French political scene.

Our examples from France and Britain have shown what a variety of political attitudes could be represented both in those movements that used the name 'Fascist', and in those which, while following their own routes, nevertheless expressed admiration for, and fellowship with, the Italian experiment. They ranged from conservative supporters of the status quo, to radical exponents of a corporatist, anti-capitalist policy; from heirs of the pre-war 'radical Right', to simple admirers of a 'firm hand' at the helm; and among them one could find racists who seemed to have more in common with the German 'völkisch' tradition.

What it is important to note, is that in France and Britain, as in the other Western democracies, such (often misleading) echoes of the Italian experiment appeared at this stage to have very little prospect of any power or success. If 'international fascism' had not achieved such importance in the Thirties, we would probably find these movements even less worthy of study than they now are. For the vast majority of politically-aware contemporaries in the Twenties, however 'radical Right' their aspirations may have been, fascism did not appear to be an alternative. In his semi-autobiographical novel *Gilles*, published in 1939, the fascist novelist Pierre Drieu la Rochelle, depicting his eponymous hero's disgust, in the late Twenties, for the contemporary political scene, makes it clear that, for those who wished to oppose bourgeois capitalism, fascism had not yet emerged as a credible alternative:

'Though I don't believe in Marxism, and even detest it with all my might, I nevertheless, just as much as the Marxists, wish to destroy present-day society. We must create a fighting force against this society, a force free of all the old doctrines, an independent force.'

At that time, when fascism was almost unknown in France (for it only became known a little at the time when it had engendered Nazism), the idea of destroying the bourgeois society could arise only in relation to Marxism. So it was with apparent justification that Lorin shrugged his shoulders.

'Outside Marxism, you will never be able to do anything.'[11]

In other countries, regimes and parties were emerging in the Twenties which, with hindsight, appeared to later commentators in the Thirties to have had some significance in relation to the subsequent growth of international fascism; to observers in the Twenties, however, they would have appeared to have little connection with what had been going on in Italy. In Romania, for example, the foundation by Corneliu Codreanu, in 1927, of the 'Legion of the Archangel Michael' (later to be known as the Iron Guard), was retrospectively to be seen as an addition to the forces of 'international fascism'. At the time, it was merely seen, and saw itself, as a highly nationalistic movement, grounded in Eastern European mysticism, anti-Semitism and authoritarianism; as with so many other movements, it was of course to view itself in a different light once the 'age of fascism' had dawned.

The 'death of fascism' outside Italy

Though, from the Thirties onwards, the impression was to gain ground that an international dimension for Fascism had existed from the start, what we have seen of the experience of the Twenties shows this to have been a fallacy. The 'publicity value' of the successes of the new regime in Italy led to an admiration for the Italian experiment in perfectly respectable political circles; it also led to a number of relatively insignificant movements, in other countries, taking up the name and the symbols of that movement, whether or not their own beliefs and policies had anything in common with it. At the same time, other elements of the pre-war 'radical Right' continued on their way, their attitude to Fascist Italy often being guarded and uncertain.

For a time in the mid-Twenties, it must be admitted, some opponents of the Right did, because of the publicity that had been given to Italy, declare all such movements to be 'fascist'; this was the first example of the vision of an international fascist threat, that was to influence fascism's development in the Thirties. Impartial observers were to draw attention to this misuse of the word and the concept. As Pierre Dominique wrote in 1927:

> The word fascism has a precise sense in Italy. It does not
> have one in France. Are M. Taittinger, M. de Kerillis, M.
> Valois and Action Française in agreement? Clearly not, yet
> the Left treats them all as being fascists.[12]

Kerillis was a leading Right-wing parliamentarian, with no
extra-parliamentary attachments; it is fascinating to see him
placed in this way alongside the leaders of Le Faisceau, the
Jeunesses Patriotes, and Action Française. Clearly, for some on
the Left, the epithet 'fascist' could already be applied to the Right
in whatever form it came.

In Germany, the Communists had been using 'fascist' as a scare-
word as early as 1923, when the Left throughout Germany staged
an 'anti-fascist' day in opposition to Germany's own versions of the
'radical Right'. But, as Ernst Nolte has pointed out, the German
Communists attached the epithet even to the moderate centre,
describing the Social Democrats as 'Social Fascists'. Matters are
made even more bewildering when we realise that groups of the
German Right, too, at about the same time, proposed calling an
'Anti-Fascist Congress'.[13] Where the Left appear to have seen
fascism as some kind of all-embracing bogey, some elements in the
Right seem to have seen it in a much narrower definition.

The idea of an international fascist threat, which appears to
have had some limited currency in the early Twenties, was
however shortlived. The lack of success of the Nazis and of other
German extreme Right-wing groups, from 1923 onwards, was
later matched by the decline, in France, for different reasons, of
the three main extra-parliamentary forces. A French police report
in August 1927 declared that 'fascism has totally disappeared
from the preoccupations of the French public [...] Neither the left-
wing press nor the conservative and reactionary press seems to be
concerned with or remember the existence of French fascism.'[14]

The Thirties were to change all this, however, and the image of
fascism was to come to loom over the whole of European life.

1. Christopher Hibbert, *Benito Mussolini*, London 1962, p. 95.
2. Note by Sir Austen Chamberlain on document C9899/1/22, Public Record
Office.

3. Press Statement from Rome, 20 January 1927, in *The Times*, 21 January 1927.

4. 'Who began Fascism in England?', *British Fascism*, 1 March 1932.

5. Arnold Leese, *Out of Step*, Guildford, 1951.

6. Arnold Leese, *Out of Step: Events in the Two Lives of an Anti-Jewish Camel-Doctor*, Guildford, 1951, p. 49.

7. Georges Valois, *L'Homme contre l'Argent, Souvenirs de dix ans, 1918-1928*, Paris 1928, p. 167.

8. Georges Valois, *Il fascismo francese*, Rome 1926, quoted in Roger Griffin, *Fascism*, Oxford University Press, 1995, pp. 197-8.

9. Robert Brasillach, *Notre Avant-guerre*, 1941. Livre de poche edition, 1992, p. 44.

10. Pierre Taittinger, *Les Cahiers de la jeune France*, 1926, quoted in Robert Soucy, *French Fascism: the First Wave, 1924-1933*, Yale University Press 1986, p. 73.

11. Pierre Drieu la Rochelle, *Gilles*, 1939. Livre de poche edition, pp. 521-2.

12. Pierre Dominique, in *Le Rappel*, quoted in Pierre Milza, *L'Italie fasciste devant l'opinion française 1920-1940*, Collection Kiosque, Armand Colin, 1967, p. 130.

13. Ernst Nolte, *Three Faces of Fascism*, Weidenfeld and Nicolson 1965, p. 3.

14. Quoted in Robert Soucy, *French Fascism: The First Wave, 1924-1933*, Yale University Press, 1986, p. 190.

Part Two

NEW DEVELOPMENTS IN
THE THIRTIES

4

The Third Way

Reactions to the Crisis of the Early Thirties

A large number of factors were to lie behind the emergence, in the early Thirties, of 'international fascism' as a major concept in European politics. Not least among these was the advent to power of the Nazis, in Germany in 1933. Well before this, however, the ground had been established upon which the new ideology (or family of ideologies) could flourish. The financial crisis which hit the whole capitalist world at the beginning of the decade played a large part in conditioning opinion-formers to believe that only radical changes in political practice could cope with the new kind of economic situation; at the same time, the social conditions created by the slump provided, at ground level, the climate in which extremist movements could flourish.

The 'Failure of Democracy', and the acceptance of totalitarian alternatives

For many observers in the early Thirties, it appeared that democratic governments were incapable of doing anything to solve the problems caused by the international economic situation. It is hard for us, nowadays, to realise the feeling of disarray in the western democracies at this time. There was a real sense of doubt, even among democracy's strongest supporters, as to its capacity to survive the crisis. This is underlined by the fact that even in Britain, the country that had probably been the least affected – in any real sense of the term – by the economic crisis, the debate was as strong as anywhere else. One has only to undertake a word-search for book-titles containing the word 'democracy', in Britain in the early Thirties, to see how uncertain democracy's future was perceived to be, even in this country: e.g., H.G. Wells, *After Democracy* (1932); H.J. Laski, *Democracy in Crisis* (1933); J.R.B. Muir, *Is Democracy a Failure?* (1934); etc.

The fact that so many countries had, since the War, moved to non-democratic governments, added to this feeling. Admiral Horthy's regency in Hungary, from 1920 onwards, had been *de facto* a dictatorship. Mussolini's rise to power in Italy in 1922 had been closely followed by that of Mustafa Kemal in Turkey in 1923. In the late twenties Marshal Pilsudski (1926) in Poland had started the trend in the eastern European states – Yugoslavia, in 1929, and Rumania, in 1931, took on forms of dictatorial government. In Portugal, the military took over in 1926, with Salazar becoming dictator in 1932. In Spain, Primo de Rivera ruled from 1923 to 1930, and appeared to many to have been far more successful than the republic that succeeded him. In 1931, the Japanese military succeeded in installing a non-democratic form of government. Other European countries (Spain, Greece, Bulgaria) were in chaos, with the threat of dictatorship looming. If one takes account of the Communist dictatorship in Russia, it must have seemed to contemporary observers that by the early Thirties few major European countries retained democratic institutions. Hitler's advent to power in Germany in 1933 merely appeared to put the seal on an already existent trend.

What made many people in the remaining democracies ask themselves whether dictatorship, in one form or another, might perhaps be the way forward, was the impression they gained that totalitarianism was better than democracy at dealing with financial crises, and that financial crises were from now on to be the major danger facing society. Of course, most of the dictatorships just mentioned had no particular virtue or success in this field; but the few that did appear to do so, were the ones that sprang to people's minds. Prominent among these was, of course, Mussolini's Italy. The Portuguese example was, however, an even more powerful one, in this respect.

When the military took over in 1926, the Portuguese economy was in a terrible mess. By 1928, the military were desperate; the country faced national bankruptcy. They appointed as Minister of Finance a professor of economics from Coimbra University called Dr António de Oliveira Salazar (1889-1970), giving him extraordinary powers. Salazar introduced a system of centralised economic controls, cut state expenditure drastically, and made use of internal loans, to such effect that by 1930 he was able to proclaim that a financial miracle had been brought about, and that Portugal's economic crisis had been solved. On the basis of the reputation that this achievement brought him, he was able to take over the premiership, as Portugal's dictator, in 1932, proclaiming his 'Estado Novo' (New State) in 1933.

Portugal's financial stability and success, at the very time when the rest of Europe appeared to be careering into economic depression, gave pause to many, and made them ask themselves whether, in order to deal with potential financial collapse, one needed to set to one side *laissez-faire* principle, and the freedom of the individual, in order to take the necessary, and often unpopular, steps to set an economy to rights. This impression was given greater weight, in the Western democracies, when the United States, reputed the greatest of the democracies, found itself considering making use of 'extraordinary powers' as, in March 1933, President Roosevelt inaugurated the 'New Deal' to solve the American economic crisis. As Roosevelt said in his radio announcement of his new measures:

> With this pledge, I assume unhesitatingly the leadership of the great army of our people dedicated to a disciplined attack upon our common problems [...] In the event that Congress should fail to take one of these two courses, and in the event that the national emergency is still critical, I shall not then evade the clear course of my duty that will then confront me.

In other words, if democracy did not work, he would have to take on dictatorial powers to solve the 'national emergency'. As is so often the case in such situations, Roosevelt then, paying lip-service to democracy, appealed over its head to an overriding 'mandate from the people':

> We do not distrust the future of essential democracy. The people of the United States have not failed. In their need they have registered a mandate that they want direct, vigorous action.

Democracy, then, was seen by many to be ineffective in face of the realities of modern life. Added to this there was the impression, in many circles, that democracy was fundamentally corrupt and self-serving; the 'virtues' of exemplary leaders could be set, in this context, against the 'morass' of parliamentary *mores*. In France, of course, this trend was particularly strong, as it had been throughout the Third Republic. Much of the popular press spent most of its time, in the early Thirties, castigating the 'louche cuisine' of parliamentarism, and calling for the 'coup de balai' that would clean it out. The widespread presumption that dictatorship was a major option is shown by a referendum held by a popular newspaper, *Le Petit Journal*, in 1934, to decide who should be the French dictator (not whether a dictatorship should be instituted; that appears to have been taken for granted). Forty names were presented to the readers, of whom 194,785 voted. Marshal Pétain won, with 38,561 votes. Pierre Laval came second, with 31,403.

Even in Britain, perfectly respectable figures could express the same weariness with democracy, and the same preoccupation with dictatorship. Sir Warden Chilcott, for example, a former Conservative MP, wrote in the *Whitehall Gazette* in 1931 that 'under the party political system' the party leaders had 'culti- vated the art of "out-Neroing Nero"', for we find them belabouring each other with bladders on sticks, whilst a country rots, and an empire disintegrates'. Chilcott declared: 'whatever form of upheaval be necessary, let us have it and get it over, and that as quickly as possible'. He expressed strong admiration for 'that great Italian patriot, Mussolini'; the position in England today was 'not wholly dissimilar' from Italy when Mussolini took over. 'Efficient resolute leadership' was imperative, for 'an army of stags led by a lion will always defeat an army of lions led by a stag.'[1]

Of course, one must stress that all these ideas about democ- racy and dictatorship did not necessarily mean that people were attracted to fascism. To most people in Britain, for example, fascism was still a foreign concept, a form of government suitable for 'lesser breeds without the law'. And totalitarianism, of course, did not necessarily mean 'fascism'. Most of the totali- tarian regimes of the Twenties had not been 'fascist' in the sense that Mussolini's Italy was. Nevertheless, the universal acceptance of the *idea* of a totalitarian solution being on the cards, and being a necessary counterbalance to the other possible solution, communism, meant that, as the Thirties progressed, the 'fascist' idea had a basis on which to build.

Intellectual acceptance of fascist policies in the early Thirties

For many figures in Western Europe, a rather naïve rejection of both Right and Left, in political terms, could lead to doctrines almost indistinguishable from those of fascism. The French Catholic philosopher Emmanuel Mounier, for example, founding his famous revue *Esprit* in 1932, came down in favour of a 'third way' which would reject both capitalism and communism, both of which were based on materialism.

Mounier is a very good example of the way in which, in the atmosphere of the early Thirties, people tended to believe that the old democratic panaceas no longer had any value. His vision was bleak:

> Events are pressing in on us. The agricultural crisis, the collapse of States, the abdication of capitalism will be with us tomorrow. Destitution is stretching out its shadow over millions of men. Before long, we will have to face up to all that. Nobody is ready technically, and up till now only communism has prepared people's will. Each one of us needs to know whether, through egoism or negligence, we will leave communism the sole inheritor.[2]

For Mounier and his companions, capitalism was the enemy – and communism was a mere offshoot of capitalism, however much it claimed to be an opponent of it. Both were the products of 'materialism':

> Our hostility is as strong with regard to capitalism, to its current practice and to its doctrine, as towards Marxism or bolshevism. Capitalism reduces a growing multitude, whether by poverty or by material well-being, to a state of slavery which is irreconcilable with the dignity of man; it orientates every class, and the whole personality of each

individual, towards the possession of money [...] Marxism is
a rebellious child of capitalism, whose faith in matter it has
inherited. Rebelling against an evil society, it carries in itself
some justice, but only until it triumphs.[3]

In face of these two enemies, Mounier's collaborators proposed a
'Third Force' in the form of a 'personalist' revolution that would
create a new world untouched by materialism.

Mounier would, of course, have rejected any connection with
'fascism'; yet nevertheless the doctrines put forward by *Esprit*,
and the movements with which Mounier and his companions
thereby found themselves in contact, steered perilously near the
'radical Right'. The rhetoric was that of fascism: the 'Third
Force' was to be 'neither Right nor Left', and the movement the
Esprit group collaborated with most closely in the early Thirties
went under the significant name of 'New Order' ('Ordre
Nouveau'). Added to this, articles in *Esprit* declared a sympathy
for the 'young national-socialists' of Germany, in face of the
corruption and materialism of the Weimar republic; and Mounier
himself, in 1935, attended a conference held in Rome by the
Institute of Fascist Culture, where, though he expressed doubts
about Fascist policies, and affirmed the fundamental differences
between his 'personalism' and Fascism, he also expressed great
enthusiasm for the people he had met, and for their 'youth,
fervour and fighting spirit', which contrasted so favourably with
'the forced, inhuman eloquence of our politicians of Right and
Left'. Even opponents of fascism, he said, had felt a 'profound
kinship' with the 'constructive vigour of these new generations'.[4]

Mounier and his friends are typical of those in the early
Thirties who, faced by the apparent failure of democracy, played
with ideas which, though apparently innocuous, were in fact very
close to the rhetoric and the reality of the radical Right. Though
they themselves could by no stretch of the imagination be called
'fascists', their naïve rejection of certain values, and acceptance
of others, meant that their views were of importance as part of
the backdrop to the increasing pro-fascism of the period.

Not all theorists of the 'Third Way' were as naïve as Mounier and
his friends. Many developed a straightforward allegiance to the
Italian model. It was in the early Thirties that some of the ground-
work laid by Mussolini's intellectual propagandists, and, more

internationally, by the enthusiasts of the CINEF, began to bear fruit. Influential thinkers in a number of Western European countries began to look specifically to the Italian example for a solution to the world's economic and political ills. In England, for example, an influential section of the Conservative Party, based around the *English Review*, had begun to show a strong interest from 1931 onwards. Douglas Jerrold, the Review's editor, was a romantic anti-capitalist Catholic in the Chestertonian tradition, who believed that 'the only serious attack on the capitalist tradition today comes from the Right'.[5] He deplored, on the one hand, the 'greedy financiers who [want] to continue the Edwardian gamble in men's lives', and on the other, 'the mass of the new trades unionists and bureaucratic planners who [want] to plant themselves securely on the taxpayer's back under the plea of public service'. What was needed, he felt, was a different kind of planning. He was attracted to a regime that had made use of the brilliant men who had been neglected by the current form of democracy, and that had righted the wrongs produced by capitalism by developing fairness within the economy. 'The Corporate State alone', he wrote, 'can combine democracy with efficiency [...] No social class, no body of political revolutionaries, neither capital nor labour nor the middle classes [...] can ever have a majority. There is no body of interested amateurs called the State to which any interest can appeal in the hope of securing, by a "bankers' ramp", or a "general strike", an advantage over its fellow interests.'[6]

Jerrold's foreign affairs contributor, Sir Charles Petrie, had produced a book entitled *Mussolini* in 1931. His admiration for the Italian dictator was to continue throughout the Thirties; he saw him as 'the greatest figure of the present age, and perhaps one of the most notable of all time'. The three main achievements of Italian Fascism, for Petrie, were the Corporate State, the solving of the Vatican problem, and the regeneration of Italy into a great power.

Other prominent Conservative journals, from the popular *Saturday Review* of Lady Houston to the more intellectual *Nineteenth Century and After*, took up the corporatist (and often pro-Mussolini) line in the period 1931-4.

The *English Review* group had aspirations to real influence of a practical kind, from which it was hoped that some introduction of corporatism into British politics might take place. In late 1933 the group provided strong support for Lord Lloyd in an attempt to oust MacDonald and Baldwin from the leadership of the National Government. Fifty or sixty MPs were interested in this challenge, the climax of which was to be an *English Review* dinner on 21 November 1933, presided over by Lord Carson. In the event, the Lloyd dinner, which 350 attended, was a resounding flop, mainly thanks, we are told, to Lloyd's character and lack of oratorical skills. But it is also possible that the differing agendas of those attending had something to do with it. While all were united in one thing, opposition to the present leadership of the National Government, most of the MPs present would have been unlikely to share the corporatist preoccupations of the *English Review* group. The dinner, and the campaign, showed the danger of the presumption that shared dislikes meant shared prescriptions for change. In the immediate aftermath of the débâcle, Jerrold came out with possibly his strongest statement on the need for a dictator, to change things:

> There is no folly more fashionable than the saying that the English will never tolerate a dictatorship. Under constitutional forms of a very flimsy character the English have invariably insisted on being governed either by a close oligarchy or a virtual dictatorship [...] It is because the party machines have notably failed to govern that they are losing the public confidence, and unless Parliament under universal franchise can fulfil the indispensable task of leadership, a dictatorship is not only inevitable but necessary.[7]

When it came to the practical achievement of fascist political ends, however, it was not the intellectual acceptance of 'Third Way' ideas, whether by French philosophers or by English Tory theoreticians, that was to have any real effect. It was the experience of the slump at ground level, by the dispossessed and the out-of-work, that created the social conditions in which fascism could thrive.

1930-33: The advent of Nazism to power

The slump did not merely produce the acceptance we have seen, among the influential classes, of the possible advantages of non-democratic government. On the ground, among the lower middle classes whose savings had been destroyed, and the workers who were affected by the mass unemployment and social hardship of this period, it created the conditions in which extremist and revolutionary movements could flourish. It was in Germany, which had already gone through the financial crash of the Twenties, that the recurrence of these conditions was to have the most dramatic effect. People turned, in despair, in both extremist directions – to the Communist Party on the Left, and to the National Socialists on the Right – until it eventually seemed that there was little place for a moderate democratic Centre.

After the failure of the Munich putsch in 1923, the Nazi Party had been in comparative decline. By 1927, it could still merely obtain between 2% and 3% of the popular vote. Even before the international slump, however, the apparently flourishing Weimar Republic had begun to be assailed by various serious economic problems. The recovery from the 1924 economic crisis had never been strong enough, and the German economy was already in a parlous state when the Wall Street crash put the seal on its misfortunes.

By 1929, the Nazis were well on the way to becoming a mass party. The Communists, too, were advancing in strength. At this stage, however, the constituencies served by the Communists and the Nazis differed from each other. The production workers who were already unemployed 'turned, in their desperation, to the KPD [the Communists]', while the middle classes turned to the Nazis, full of 'fear of economic hardship, fear of loss of social status – which led to hopelessness, despair, and finally willingness to support any party that combined familiar appeals to traditional values with promises of immediate relief.'[8] The party welcomed, in the deteriorating economic situation of late 1929, a large number of salaried white-collar workers as new members.

In the elections of September 1930, the Nazis polled 18.3%, the Communists 13.1%. Proportional representation meant that each had a considerable position in the parliament (the Nazis getting 107 seats). Meanwhile, outside parliamentary politics, the street gangs of both Right and Left began to dominate the national life.

On 1 June 1932 Franz von Papen (1879-1969), a traditional reactionary, had been appointed Chancellor by President

Hindenburg. He introduced a series of measures that, by weakening parliamentary democracy, might almost seem to have been paving the way for an eventual Nazi takeover. His aim appears to have been to unite the traditional Right in face of the threat from the Left, by instituting a more authoritarian regime. His first action was to dissolve the Reichstag (the parliament), and institute new elections in July.

In the July 1932 elections, the Nazis polled 37.3% of the votes cast, and became the largest party in the parliament. Hitler's opportunity was to come mainly through the lack of insight of Papen and the traditional Right. Papen, who had been overwhelmingly defeated in a Reichstag vote, resigned as Chancellor on 17 November 1932. Eager to retrieve his position, he looked around him for a potential ally – and perceived Hitler and the Nazis. Feeling that he and his colleagues could easily keep in check this upstart politician, while making use of his parliamentary votes, Papen held secret talks with Hitler and President Hindenburg in January 1933. The deal that they hammered out involved Hitler being appointed Chancellor, with Papen as Vice-Chancellor. Rarely has such a political miscalculation been made as Papen's belief that he could control Hitler.

Hitler was appointed Chancellor on 30 January 1933. His Cabinet contained only two other Nazis, Goering and Frick, and it must have seemed to Hindenburg and Papen that he was properly hemmed in by conservatives. But they were mistaken. Because the parliamentary alliance still did not have an overall majority, Hitler used his first Cabinet meeting to decide on new elections, to take place on 5 March. In the meantime, the Reichstag fire on 27 February gave him the excuse to bring in emergency laws, aimed at temporarily removing constitutional rights and safeguards. These temporary powers were to become permanent, destroying what was left of democracy in Germany.

The March election was marked by wholesale intimidation and violence, accompanied by scare propaganda based on the Communist threat as 'revealed' by the Reichstag fire. In it the Nazis obtained 43.9% of the vote, which translated into 288 seats. Hitler could now consolidate his power without need of the conservative parliamentary forces which had eased his way up to now. He was to remain aware, however, of the need to conserve a wide range of Right-wing support, and a number of his policies and actions in the years to come were to be aimed at reassuring, and playing down the 'revolutionary' elements in pre-power Nazism.

From March 1933 onwards, the Nazi State was fully in being.

The emergence of other movements

It would be wrong to see, as has often been suggested, the emergence of the Nazi Party in 1930-33 as being the only major catalyst for all the other manifestations of the European 'revolutionary Right' in those years. Of course, as we shall see, once the Nazis were in power, from 1933 onwards, the impact of their example was to be considerable in other European countries; but in the early Thirties the conditions favourable to authoritarian movements were such, that many such movements grew up alongside, and entirely independent of, Nazism. Indeed, the stimulus for most of them appears to have been either Mussolini's Fascism, or (paradoxically, when AF was in comparative decline in France) Maurras's Action Française.

Typical of those movements inspired by Mussolini was, in Britain, the British Union of Fascists, founded in 1932 by Sir Oswald Mosley (1896-1980). Like so many such movements, its origins lay on the Left. Mosley was Chancellor of the Duchy of Lancaster in the Labour Government that had been formed in 1929. In 1930 he produced a Memorandum, heavily influenced by Keynesian theories, which made radical recommendations for economic recovery, involving state intervention and a public works programme. When this was rejected by the Cabinet, he resigned his Ministry in May 1930, and in March 1931 he left the Labour Party, launching his New Party. At first this party was conceived entirely in parliamentary terms. Mosley and four other MPs (3 Labour, 1 Conservative) remained in Parliament under the new banner. Discussions about alliances took place, and Mosley hoped for at least a dozen seats in the elections of October 1931. The election results were, however, disastrous, and all 24 New Party candidates were defeated. This convinced Mosley that his solutions to the national situation could not be furthered by parliamentary means. After a visit to Italy in early 1932, he set about creating a British Fascist movement. In the 1932 situation, when so many people were predicting the demise of democracy,

Mosley now saw the future as lying with a dictatorial system which, alone, could solve the problems of the modern economy. On 1 October 1932 the British Union of Fascists was launched. This was a movement which, even though it was never to come anywhere near the prospect of power, was of a completely different order from the British experiments of the nineteen-twenties; at its height, in 1933-4, it had a considerable following, and despite a subsequent decline in support, remained a prominent thorn in the flesh of the authorities right up to the internment of many of its members in May 1940.

It is interesting to note, however, how many of the movements of these years, in Europe and beyond, found their inspiration in the old French model of Action Française. This will give particular importance to our eventual discussion of the debate over the 'fascist' or 'non-fascist' nature of this French movement. In Portugal, where the Integralists had, from 1914 onwards, based their doctrines on AF principles, the Salazar dictatorship, which was formalised in 1932, equally owed allegiance to the teachings of Maurras.

Maurras's policies were particularly attractive to movements which combined anxieties at the economic situation with specifically nationalist, or religious, concerns. Other movements emerging in 1930-33 which owed some at least of their policies to Maurras included, in Belgium, Van Severen's Flemish nationalist 'Verbond van Dietsche Nationaalsolidaristen' (League of Dutch-speaking Workers for National Solidarity) and Léon Degrelle's Catholic 'Rex' movement, formally founded in the mid-Thirties, but already there in embryo from 1930 onwards; in Spain, from 1931, Maeztu's 'Hispanism', whose mouthpiece was the significantly-named 'Acción Española'; and even, in Brazil, the equally aptly named 'Brazilian Integralist Action' founded in 1932 by Plinio Salgado, which by 1934 had an active membership of about 200,000. This Action Française influence in other countries was to continue right through the Thirties, alongside the more expected influences of Nazism and Italian Fascism; Metaxas's dictatorship in Greece, from 1936 onwards, for example, was heavily influenced by Maurras's doctrines.

The move towards dictatorship, or towards movements promoting authoritarian doctrines, did not, therefore, in the period 1930-33, necessarily base itself on the example of Italian

Fascism, or of German Nazism. It was only as the decade proceeded that all such tendencies began to be tarred with the same brush, as 'international fascism' became an overriding concept both for supporters and for opponents of such movements. We shall be examining, later, the complexities of this situation.

1. Articles in *Whitehall Gazette*, January and April 1931, reprinted in Sir Warden Chilcott, *Political Salvation 1930-32*, London, 1932.
2. Mounier, 'Programme for 1933', *Esprit*, December 1932.
3. Prospectus of *Esprit*, February 1932, quoted in Sternhell, *Ni droite ni gauche*, p. 305.
4. Quoted in Sternhell, op.cit., p. 308.
5. Douglas Jerrold, *Georgian Adventure*, 1937, p. 313.
6. Douglas Jerrold, 'The Corporate State in England', *Everyman*, 13 October 1933.
7. Douglas Jerrold, 'Current Comments', *English Review*, December 1933.
8. Dietrich Orlow, *History of the Nazi Party, Vol. I, 1919-1933*, David and Charles, 1971, p. 175.

'Firm Leaders not Drift'

The Years 1933-6 and the Emergence of the Concept of International Fascism

Nazism in power

Within weeks of the Nazi Party's success in the March 1933 elections, Hitler put before the Parliament a proposal for the Government to have direct powers to rule by decree. The necessary two-thirds majority was ensured by various forms of threat and coercion. Shortly thereafter the parliaments of the federal States were dismissed, and Commissioners appointed to rule in their place, 'in order to maintain order'. Within three months all political parties except the Nazi party had ceased to exist. A year later, at the death of Hindenburg, Hitler abolished the post of President, and from now on was Head of State as well as Chancellor.

Two of the main distinguishing marks of the new regime were the contrasting ones of repression of potential enemies and minorities, and conciliation of other groups that posed potential threats. So, on the one hand, left-wingers were purged, and the first concentration camps set up; on the other, a Concordat was signed with the Vatican in July 1933, by which, in return for religious freedom, the bishops took an oath of loyalty to the State, and Catholic political action ceased. Like most revolutionaries who come to power, Hitler soon realised the need for support from the very areas that he had previously scorned. To achieve majority support in the nation, he needed to appeal to conservatives as well as radicals; to forge a successful economy he needed the support of big business; to be safe in power, he needed first to obtain the support of the army, and then to neutralise it as a political force.

The Night of the Long Knives, in July 1934, appears above all to have been aimed at the reassurance of those elements in society whose support he so critically needed. The SA, which had been so instrumental in eliminating serious political opposition to the Nazis from the streets, was seen by many of Hitler's potential new allies as standing for the 'disreputable' side of the Nazi movement before its achievement of power. Added to this, Ernst Roehm, Chief of Staff of the SA, had begun declaring his movement's dissatisfaction with Hitler's apparent abandonment of the aim of radically restructuring society. The Nazi leadership, fearing the prospect of further revolutionary activity, and aware of the 'bad press' that Roehm and his followers were bringing to the Party among those it now wished to impress, urged Hitler to get rid of him. In a surprise move, Hitler used the SS to murder Roehm and a number of his closest SA lieutenants.

The 'economic miracle' that Hitler appeared to achieve in the years 1933-9 was brought about mainly through collaboration with German big business, through the rearmament programme, and through Keynesian measures, including a public expenditure programme on such things as the Autobahns (the first motorways). The conditions were created in which this could all work, for a time at least (what would have happened in the longer term is less certain – but the longer term was never to materialise).

The economic recovery was, of course, a major factor in the growing popularity of Hitler. The solving of the unemployment problem not only brought the Nazis great support among the workers; it also played a large part in the favourable impression made by the new regime in many circles abroad, in such countries as France and Britain, where the 'excesses' of Nazism were, by many, claimed to be disappearing, as the regime 'matured'. Hitler's popularity within Germany, however, stemmed from a number of other causes as well. Among these were his aggressive foreign policy, and the restoration of 'national self-respect'. The imagery and atmosphere of the regime, too, were very influential. People were bowled over by the great events, including the Nuremberg Rallies, with their massive and emotive pageantry. And then there was the 'cult of youth', with its emphasis on virile companionship and national values. The Hitler Youth organisation, which had been founded in the nineteen-twenties, concentrated on military-style training, and aroused enormous enthusiasm among the young, eventually attracting over 6 million members.

Amid all this euphoria, many Germans appear either to have failed to notice the darker side of the regime under which they existed, or to have approved of it. Within the first year of Nazi government, a repressive state apparatus had been developed, based on the SS and the Gestapo (State Secret Police), in which all questioning of the regime and its activities was severely dealt with. The concentration camps which grew up were at this stage used mainly for communists and opponents of the regime; it was not until later that their prime purpose became that of anti-Jewish repression.

One of the Nazi Party's most potent attractions, in its ascent to power, had been its rabid anti-Semitic propaganda, which provided a convenient scapegoat for all the ills being suffered by the German people. In the prevailing middle-European culture, both in Germany and in countries further East, such propaganda found a fertile breeding-ground in many areas of society. Hitler's anti-Semitism, however, was based on far more radical racial theories than mere 'anti-capitalist' anti-Semitism, and, though the measures at first taken against the Jews seemed to be mainly economic (exclusion from various forms of employment, other economic sanctions, and various forms of social exclusion), the underlying racial violence remained.

One must not underestimate the seriousness of the Jewish situation from the start. Alongside the foaming utterances of Julius Streicher's paper *Der Stürmer*, an atmosphere of hatred for the Jews permeated German society. Though favourable outside observers commented, in the first years, on the new 'moderation' to be perceived in the Nazis now that they were in power, as early as March 1933 a boycott against Jewish businesses, lawyers, doctors, etc., was legalised. In 1935 the Nuremberg Laws defined 'Jewishness', forbade sexual relations between Aryans and Jews, and withdrew citizenship from Jews. Jewish existence in the new Germany became one of exclusion and harassment. Violence towards the Jews in the streets, whether by the SS or by ordinary citizens, became commonplace. Aware of the anxieties felt by other countries about such policies, the Nazis produced what has been called the 'Olympic pause' in 1936, whereby anti-Semitism was played down, and no major speeches on the subject made. The pause was a short one, however. The Nazis soon began once more their policy of exclusion of the Jews from all significant walks of life, of taking over Jewish assets cheaply and under threat, and of producing violent anti-Jewish propaganda from official and unofficial sources. Anti-Semitism, which had from the start been a major plank in the Nazi Party's platform, continued to be one of its major defining features. While the threat to Jewish lives was not as clear as it was to become, the violence of Nazi anti-Semitism could, even at this stage, hardly be ignored by the rest of the world.

The spread of the idea of 'international fascism'

Although we have seen a number of new movements of the 'radical Right' appearing in the period 1930-33, some under the influence of Mussolini's Italy, and others under the influence of Action Française, it appears to have been the advent of the Nazis to power in Germany that sparked off the generalised idea of 'international fascism', an idea that was to dominate the next twelve years. What had been disparate movements now appeared to be part of a more coherent whole, and a polarisation of European politics between 'antifascists' and 'fascists' began to take place. As a result, events that might have seemed local, and typical of previous experience, began to take on the appearance of being part of that international polarisation (for example, the French riots of 6 February 1934, and the Spanish Civil War); and, of course, as so often happens, a reality then formed itself from what had at first been mere appearance. Eventually, the 'fascist age' took form in reality as well as in myth.

But, to start with the new perception of fascism as an international force: from what quarter did this new concept come? Its invention has often been ascribed to opponents of Nazism and of the radical Right; but it has also to be said that members of that dispersed radical Right, fortified by the Nazi success, also began to see themselves as being part of an international brotherhood. It is difficult to know which came first, the cart or the horse. Be that as it may, each group fed off the other, to create what Sorel would no doubt have described as a 'healthy' tension.

The contribution of the Left to the creation of the myth

In his memoirs Robert Brasillach, later to be one of the most prominent French fascists, gave his own interpretation of the way in which the idea of 'international fascism' had first impressed itself upon people in France. It was, he said, as a direct result of the Nazi advent to power in 1933; but it was not an idea produced by 'fascists' themselves. It was an idea forged, in his view, by the refugees from Germany:

> Driven out pell-mell, whether Jews or socialists, they began to build in France a vast Wailing Wall, before which they called the whole world to witness. [...] And they also brought with them a monster, a phantom, the shadow of International Fascism; against the Red International they set, vehemently, a White International which was the cause of all evils, and they denounced, in the slightest authoritarian doctrine, an enormous totalitarian heresy, ready to take over the universe. Up till then, Fascism had been Italy, which was detested, but an individual case. In 1933, the 'accursed doctrine' had taken possession of the old country of Revolution, the native soil of Marxism. It was only then that people began to perceive that Portugal, Poland, Lithuania, were living under dictatorships. [...] The refugees [...] did their best to collaborate in the creation of the very terror they were denouncing. One could already perceive, right across Europe, the beginning of a War of Religion that was to last for more than five years.[1]

By the late Thirties Brasillach was to be one of the most fervent Right-wing supporters of the concept of 'international fascism', so it is interesting to see him placing the initial responsibility for this concept on its opponents. And, though Brasillach's vision of what had happened is clearly partial, it represents an over-simplified version of a basic truth: that fear of the new 'international force' was to play a large part in the politics of the Left and of the Centre in the next few years.

The Communist International had reacted strongly against Italian Fascism in the early Twenties. By the late Twenties, aware of the rise of the threat of Nazism in Germany, it had begun to classify all political regimes which upheld capitalism, from Fascism to Social Democracy, as 'fascists'. However, though at its first session after the Nazi seizure of power, in December 1933, it accepted that a new international threat had emerged, the delegates still refused to contemplate any alliance with the 'social fascists' of Social Democracy against the dictatorial fascism which they now perceived not only in Germany, but also in the old-established dictatorships of such countries as Portugal and Poland. This refusal to work with potential democratic allies against the 'fascist threat' was not, however, to last. One of the major achievements of the new left-wing vision of 'international fascism' was to create the situation whereby a series of widely-based coalitions of the Left could, while initially formed to face up to that threat, in fact achieve real political power.

The communist objection to working with democratic parties was based not only on principle, but also on pragmatism. A revolutionary party going into partnership with democratic parties was bound to have to compromise, to abandon certain policies in order to fit in with its partners, and in the process to water down its commitment to the major concerns of the proletariat.

Eventually, it was in France that the Comintern's original policy was resoundingly to be reversed. This was largely as a result of the famous riots of 6 February 1934, which were a prime case of the 'fascist myth' being used to transform events which, when viewed objectively, seem to have had other perfectly explicable causes.

6 February 1934

Though they are now almost forgotten outside France, the events of 6 February 1934 in Paris appeared, to contemporaries inside and outside France, to be one of the decisive moments of the inter-war period. Yet, if one looks at it closely, the demonstration that took place on that day only differed from many others that had, over the years, been undertaken by the French extra-parliamentary Right, in two respects: (i) there was greater collaboration between the Right-wing groups; (ii) the governmental reaction caused a number of deaths, at the hands of the police.

As with so many Right-wing demonstrations against the Third Republic, from the late nineteenth century onwards, this one had been caused by popular discontent at revelations of financial corruption. The Stavisky scandal, which had been brewing since late 1933, had come to a head, and it was clear that ministers and parliamentarians had been involved. This, to which could be added a succession of financial crises since the 1932 elections, and the impressions of muddled parliamentarism and horse-trading created by governmental attempts at reshuffling and compromise after the resignation of the Chautemps government at the end of January, appeared to present a good opportunity for a public demonstration of strength by the Right. The 6 February was preceded by several days of lesser riots. For the day itself, a number of groups co-ordinated to the extent of deciding to act at the same time; but each group in fact pursued its own demonstration. The main groups involved were the Croix de Feu (an extreme right-wing movement of ex-servicemen), the Jeunesses Patriotes, the National Union of Ex-Servicemen, and of course Action Française. Those concerned were therefore a mixture of the radical and the more traditional Right, and consisted in large part of disgruntled ex-servicemen appalled by parliamentary incompetence and dishonesty. Their aim appears to have been to *protest*, and possibly to bring the *government* of the day down; it does not seem to have been to bring the *regime* down in a revolutionary manner. The historian René Rémond has described it as 'a street manifestation that went wrong', and as 'a Boulangist demonstration rather than the March on Rome'.[2] It was, in fact, an anti-parliamentary riot which because of overreaction by the authorities, and excessive bloodshed, was made to seem more important than it in fact was.

And yet this soon came to be described as an attempted 'fascist putsch'. One has to ask oneself, however, to what extent the participants in such a 'putsch' would have been as content as the rioters turned out to be, with what resulted from that day's events. Though the Daladier Government resigned, this was no blow to the Republican regime; and the subsequent appointment of a sound old Centre-Right Republican, Gaston Doumergue, to head a Government of National Unity, while clearly designed to reassure the public, and to placate the Right, cannot be seen as any kind of response to an attempted 'putsch' to overthrow the regime. The groups of 6 February were not an organised attempt to change things by force, but a forcible and negative expression of disapproval, such as the radical Right had often mounted in the past.

As was so often to happen from now on, however, the Left reacted to the bogey of 'international fascism'. Up till now, of course, the Soviet policy of non-collaboration with other parties of the Left had been in force. In the immediate aftermath of 6 February, the prominent French communist Jacques Doriot (1898-1945), already doubtful about the Comintern line, called for immediate talks with the SFIO (the Socialist Party), in order to form 'a united front against fascism'. His rival for the party Leadership, Maurice Thorez, a Soviet 'apparachik', continued to take the Moscow line. With Moscow's approval, Doriot was expelled from the Party. Yet the irony was that, the moment he had left, the French party, with Moscow's permission, changed its line, and Doriot's proposed policy was implemented in his absence. The direct result of this was to be the 'Front Populaire' alliance of July 1935 between Communists, Socialists and Radicals, which was to sweep the polls in 1936, bringing in the first truly Left-wing government of the Third Republic.

The result for Doriot is well known. He maintained his position as mayor of the Communist fief of St Denis, and, now filled with hatred of communism, formed a new party in July 1936. This party, the Parti Populaire Français (French People's Party), has generally been regarded as 'fascist'.

If the Left was happy to see 6 February as a 'fascist putsch', the Right was even more happy to do so. The new 'fascists' forgot the faulty organisation, the lack of any clear goal, which had marked the day, and thrilled to the sense of a real fascist revolution, even though that 'revolution' had failed. In his novel *Gilles* (1939), the fascist writer Drieu la Rochelle (1893-1945), describes the reactions of his hero Gilles on the day itself:

> But you don't realise what's going on. This people is not dead, as we have all believed, this people has arisen from its bed of torpor. [...] It's the first time I have been alive, for twenty years [...] Now, I'll march with whoever will bloody well knock this regime down, on any conditions.[3]

In another retrospective piece of fiction, the 1940 *Les Captifs*, Robert Brasillach describes his hero Gilbert returning from the events of the day, and writing in his diary as he goes to bed: '6 February 1934 – Year One of the National Revolution'. The 'National Revolution' was one of the catchwords of the radical Right, coined by Georges Valois in the Twenties. By juxtaposing this with a reference to the Revolutionary Calendar from the French Revolution, Brasillach was suggesting that, at the time, participants saw the 6 February as a 'revolutionary' event. Both Drieu's and Brasillach's accounts were, of course, retrospective; but there is little doubt that, even if the 6 February was not a 'fascist putsch', it swiftly became so in the minds of a number of the young radical Right – to the extent that, in its immediate aftermath, Drieu la Rochelle wrote an enthusiastic book *Socialisme fasciste* (Fascist Socialism) (1934) in which he declared that the failure of 6 February had shown that the only solution for France was the creation of a party on the model of the successful ones in Italy and Germany, a national socialist party.

Brasillach, too, accepted the failure of the 6th. For him, however, a myth remained, that summed up all that 'fascist youth' were aspiring to. Brasillach agreed that it had been an 'unsuccessful plot'; but he praised it in emotional words which sum up something of the romanticism of certain fascists:

> But even if the 6th was an unsuccessful plot, it was an instinctive and magnificent revolt, it was a night of sacrifice, which remains in our memories with its smell, its cold wind, its pale running figures, its human groups on the pavements, its invincible hope in a National Revolution, the birth of national socialism in our country. What does it matter if everything ended up by being exploited by Right and Left, everything of that burning fire, of those dead who were pure. No-one can prevent what has been from having been.[4]

So, for both Right and Left in France, the events of 6 February 1934 became an exemplary lesson. To the Left, it became the bogey of an 'international fascist' plot, and a spur to 'antifascist' action; to the Right, it became a great example of a 'new age' of fascism, which had become not just a national, but a European phenomenon. This is but one example of the new attitudes which the Nazi advent to power had brought about; throughout the Thirties events were to be interpreted according to this new viewpoint.

The Right, for and against the concept of a 'fascist international'

In the Twenties the success of Fascist Italy had not, as we have seen, produced any significant sense of an international movement which might develop from it. There were other movements which had some similarities with it, in other countries in Europe. Some were based on the pre-war 'radical Right' model; others, including Nazism, were based on a middle-European 'völkisch' model. And various kinds of dictatorship, many of them apparently unconnected with the 'radical Right', had also come into existence in this period. But the only movements which had openly claimed a relationship to Italian Fascism had been of widely differing nature, often misinterpreting the nature of their model, and politically insignificant. In the early Thirties, on the other hand, the social and economic situation had favoured the emergence of a variety of new 'radical Right' movements across Europe, mostly based either on the model of Italian Fascism, or on that of Action Française. But it was the advent to power of a totally different movement, German Nazism, that produced, paradoxically, the idea that all these movements formed part of an international whole.

The reactions of the Right were in fact mixed. For a large number of people, the concept of a new international force was an exhilarating one, and they perceived a new spirit, summed up in the idea of 'fascist man', 'homo fascista'. In the process, while aware of the incidental differences between the various movements they saw as part of this new 'International', they stressed the 'new spirit' which lay behind them all (conveniently fitting already existent movements into the new pattern):

Italy was the first to realise a doctrine that was both nationalist and social [...] Then, Oliveira Salazar's Portugal, founded on Christian principles, gave us the model of a corporative system inspired by La Tour du Pin [...] When Germany in her turn had accomplished her revolution, she brought to it her own personality [...] We saw the flame light up almost everywhere, we saw the old world being gradually threatened. It was, amid the plains and canals of Holland, Mussert's *National-socialistische Beweging*; it was, in the suburbs of London itself, Oswald Mosley's *British Union of Fascists* [...] it was the Swiss nationalists; all the peoples in their turn, from Greece and the Balkans to the Norwegian fjords, and to the red plains of Castile, began a long night of agitated insomnia, where they, each in their own way, heard the song: 'Nation, awake!'. In Roumania, Corneliu Codreanu addressed his legionnaires in speeches full of tough, colourful rhetoric [...] And in Belgium, land of traditional liberalism, Rexism accentuated, because of its thirty-year-old leader, the most spectacular and attractive feature of this new world: youth. The world blazed, the world sang, and united, the world set to work.[5]

We can note that among the movements listed there are a number which, in the Twenties and early Thirties, had seemed to have little debt to Italian Fascism; and that now, in the aftermath of Nazism's fantastic success, the German 'völkisch' tradition appears as part of the same universal package.

If, on the one hand, already existent movements were now reclassified as 'fascist', from 1933 onwards a number of movements that were already 'fascist' took on, more and more, the German model. Some took on the name 'national socialist', such as Mussert's Dutch movement, which has just been referred to; and eventually, in 1936, Mosley's British Union of Fascists, having swung violently into anti-Semitism in late 1934, took on an additional title, as the 'British Union of Fascists and National Socialists'.

The German model was most assiduously followed, however, in Scandinavia and in Eastern Europe, and, as might have been expected, contained liberal doses of racism and anti-Semitism. In Norway, Vidkun Quisling's 'Nasjonal Samling', founded in 1933, called for an alliance of all 'Nordic' peoples against the 'Jewish' forces of Communism. In Finland, the 'Isänmaallinen Kansanliike' (People's Patriotic Movement), which called for a Greater Finland, equally associated the Jews with Communism. In Latvia the 'Perkonkrust' (Thunder Cross) movement, which was later to serve the Nazis so dutifully when Germany occupied the Baltic States, turned its nationalistic fervour against all ethnic minorities, but particularly against the Jews.[6]

In Western Europe, however, despite the attraction of the idea of a more universal fascism, the German connection stuck in the throat of a number of the admirers of the Italian experiment. Not everyone shared the view that Nazism was just one more example of Fascism. In England, for example, the editorial policy of Jerrold's *English Review* and Lady Houston's *Saturday Review* appears to have been to continue to praise Fascist Italy, while attacking Nazi Germany, which was seen as completely different. Douglas Jerrold, while continuing in vocal support for Mussolini, declared how appalled he was by the 'revival of the persecution of the Jews', and felt that it had 'irreparably damaged the prestige of the new regime in this country'. Incidentally, this shows how little fascism had, until this time, been associated, by such people, with anti-Semitism.

But it was not just Nazi anti-Semitism that led many on the Right to distinguish between Nazism and Italian Fascism. Sir Charles Petrie, in a series of articles in 1933-4, found little in common between the two movements (whereas, in his book *Lords of the Inland Sea* (1937), he was to stress the similarity of the various Mediterranean experiments). Though, he claimed, 'Hitler would not have succeeded but for the achievements of Mussolini', any resemblance between the two movements was accidental. 'They both represent the reaction against the old democratic order, and that is all'. Not only was it 'an impertinence to put Hitler in the same category as Mussolini', it was also clear that the movements differed entirely. 'It is difficult to believe that the Nazi movement is much more than the old Prussianism in a new form', he wrote. Fascism stood for the legacy of Roman civilisation, 'for the family, for religion, and for discipline'. None of this had any appeal for the Nazis, 'who would apply eugenic tests to the relations of the sexes, who wish religion to be a department of State, and who appear to prefer emotionalism to the practice of self-control'. The Nazis stood for 'considered cynicism and ruthless egotism'; they had 'no great European sense', unlike Fascism, which was 'in the main stream of the great European tradition'; and even if there was much that was commendable in the Nazi wish to purify their country after fifteen years of Socialism, their methods were 'deplorable'.[7]

Similarly France's Henri Massis, a fervent admirer of Mussolini, Salazar and Franco, felt that Hitlerism was wrongly associated with fascism:

> Even though it lays claim to doing so, Hitlerism could in no way be taken for a defence of Western civilisation. Even though it mimics that civilisation's notions of order, hierarchy and authority, it repudiates its major ideas, its fundamental doctrines, and it denounces them as tendencies that are fatal to the German genius.

Massis spoke against 'the excesses of German racism', 'the doctrines of force, of violence, created by destructive Germanism'. This, he implied, had nothing to do with 'fascism'. In fascism, on the contrary, he saw 'noble, elevated virtues that we Frenchmen are fitted more than anyone else to esteem and admire'. To confuse that with the German regime seemed to him, even as late as 1939, to be 'a blind, unjust procedure'.[8]

In the same way, in Spain, Ernesto Giménez Caballero, in the year before the Nazis' accession to power, had told Spanish youth, in his book *Genio de España* (1932), to distinguish between the pagan fascism of the Nazis and Mussolini's 'Christian fascism'.[9] It is significant that most of the observers who distinguished between the movements in this way were Catholics who did so on a religious basis; we shall be looking more closely into this question of 'Catholic fascism' in a later chapter.

It is only with hindsight that we see the choices to be made in the Thirties as having been simple ones. There were, among outside observers, many who approved of one aspect of 'international fascism', and disliked others. There was no necessary correlation between pro-Fascism and pro-Nazism. One could be pro-Mussolini and anti-Hitler, pro-Franco after 1936 and neither pro-Mussolini nor pro-Hitler. France's Georges Bernanos, a fervent Right-winger, could on the other hand abhor Franco and his followers, and have some sympathy for Hitler.

On one thing everyone nevertheless seems to have been agreed: there was such a thing as 'international fascism', and various historical events were clearly manifestations of it. The

Spanish Civil War is a very good example of how this state of mind took over, to the extent that, eventually, the myth became reality.

The Spanish Civil War

The Spanish Civil War, which broke out in 1936, appeared at first to be the product of a situation typical of Spain over the past century and a half. In face of what was seen as civil chaos, the Army had declared that it was taking over power. The only difference was, that the resistance was such that matters were prolonged into a long and bloody civil war.

Despite all this, for most contemporaries the Spanish Civil War came to represent the battleground between the two major political forces between which Europe appeared to be divided. Victory for one's enemies would mean either the victory of 'fascism' or that of 'communism'.

For the Left, and for the Right, it was easy to see the other side as being a monolithic entity, on both the Spanish and the European level. Sections of the British and French Right, for example, saw the whole Republican side as some kind of 'Bolshevik conspiracy'. Added to that, one of the strongest claims made about the War, by supporters of Franco, was that it was a Christian crusade against the anti-Christian excesses of the Republicans. There was thus a widespread Catholic commitment to Franco's side, which combined anti-Bolshevism with religious fervour.

For the Left, on the other hand, the Spanish Nationalists represented a part of the onward march of fascism throughout Europe. It was for this reason that so many volunteers came forward for the International Brigade. C. Day Lewis described the struggle in Spain as 'part of a conflict going on now all over the world, 'a battle between light and darkness', and W.H. Auden put the case even more starkly:

I support the Valencia Government in Spain because its defeat by the forces of International Fascism would be a major disaster for Europe. It would make a European War far more probable; and the spread of Fascist Ideology and practice to countries as yet comparatively free from them, which would inevitably follow upon a Fascist victory in Spain, would create an atmosphere in which the creative artist and all who care for justice, liberty and culture would find it impossible to exist.*[10]

On the other side, a conservative French writer like Paul Claudel saw the Spanish Republican cause as being a front for the establishment of a Communist state on France's southern frontier. Railing against Soviet Russia in an article deploring the Franco-Soviet Pact, he wrote:

It is with this tyranny, it is with this people of torturers and slaves, that conservative France, thanks to M. Louis Barthou, concluded this pact. And it is this same régime that the Azañas and the Caballeros, aided by Moscow, have been endeavouring to establish on our doorstep.[11]

While, at the outset, there was little to associate the Spanish military uprising with 'international fascism', or the Left-wing Republican government and its supporters with 'international communism', it is also clear that, once the myth-making had begun, the situation itself changed. Once Spain became seen as the international battleground between the two major forces that were already obsessing Europe, it actually became such a battleground. In the process, the 'fascist' Powers, Germany and Italy, intervened on Franco's side with forces and resources, and the Soviets sent advisers to the Republican side. The myth became reality.

Nowhere are contemporary attitudes clearer than in the literature of the Spanish Civil War. Throughout André Malraux's novel *L'Espoir* (1939), for example, which was written entirely

* On the tangential question of artistic liberty, it is worth noting that, in John Butt's words, in the Thirties 'The Left was, as is well known, more systematically intolerant of artistic and literary modernism than the Right. Deliberate attacks on Modernism had been coming from the Communists and their fellow travellers since before the first All-Union Congress of Soviet Writers in Moscow in 1934, where socialist realism was defined as dogma.' (Butt, 'Modernism and the Anti-Democratic Right in Spain', in *The Pen and the Sword: Right-wing Politics and Literary Innovation in the twentieth Century*, ed. Richard Griffiths, 2000, p.42).

from the Republican standpoint, the Republic's opponents the Nationalists are described as 'les fascistes'; and the same holds true of the attitudes of all the writers, French or English, who wrote about the war from the Republican side.

But 'international fascism', whether an invention of its opponents or of its supporters, had by now taken on a life of its own. Members of the 'radical Right' in a wide variety of countries began to perceive themselves as part of a vast international movement, and any differences they might perceive were soon glossed over. The Rexist José Streel, for example, hailed the force that had 'welled up' out of the very substance of the peoples of the world, and which had created the 'revolution of the twentieth century'.[12]

Some people were, however, already beginning to be concerned by the widespread and ill-defined use of the word 'fascist'. Evelyn Waugh, in a letter to *The New Statesman* in 1938, deplored the devaluation of the word in terms that are surprisingly modern to our ears:

There was a time in the early twenties when the word 'Bolshie' was current. It was used indiscriminately of refractory schoolchildren, employees who asked for a rise in wages, impertinent domestic servants, those who advocated an extension of the rights of property to the poor, and anything or anyone of whom the speaker disapproved. The only result was to impede reasonable discussion and clear thought.

I believe we are in danger of a similar, stultifying use of the word 'Fascist'. There was recently a petition sent to English writers [...] asking them to subscribe themselves, categorically, as supporters of the Republican Party in Spain, or as 'Fascists'. When rioters are imprisoned it is described as a 'Fascist sentence'; the Means Test is Fascist; colonization is Fascist; military discipline is Fascist; patriotism is Fascist; Catholicism is Fascist; Buchmanism is Fascist; the ancient Japanese cult of their Emperor is Fascist; fox-hunting is Fascist ... Is it too late to call for order? [...] There is a highly nervous and highly vocal party who are busy creating a bogy; if they persist in throwing an epithet about it may begin to stick.[13]

1. Robert Brasillach, *Notre Avant-guerre*, Paris, Plon, 1941. Livre de poche edition, 1992, pp. 174-5.

2. René Rémond, *La Droite en France*, Paris, Aubier, 1963, pp. 216-7.

3. Drieu la Rochelle, *Gilles*, 1939, Folio edition, pp. 596-600.

4. Robert Brasillach, *Notre Avant-guerre*, pp. 151-2.

5. Ibid., pp. 303-4.

6. See extracts from the pronouncements of these movements, in Roger Griffin, *Fascism*, OUP 1995, pp. 208-18

7. Sir Charles Petrie, 'Current Comments', *English Review*, April 1933, and 'Fascism and the Nazis', *Saturday Review*, 20 May 1933.

8. Henri Massis, *Chefs*, Paris, Plon, 1939, pp. 9, 23, 27, 39.

9. Quoted in John Butt, 'Modernism and the Anti-Democratic Right in Spain', in *The Pen and the Sword: Right-Wing Politics and Literary Innovation in the Twentieth Century*, ed. Richard Griffiths, London, Centre for Twentieth-Century Cultural Studies, 2000.

10. Lewis and Auden texts taken from *Authors Take Sides in the Spanish War*, Lawrence and Wishart, 1937.

11. Paul Claudel, 'Une saison en enfer', *Nouvelle Revue Française*, 1 August 1938.

12. José Streel, *La Révolution du vingtième siècle*, Brussels 1942, quoted in Griffin, op.cit., p. 206.

13. Evelyn Waugh, Letter to *New Statesman and Nation*, 5 March 1938.

Part Three

THE MYTH BECOMES REALITY: THE NATURE OF 'FASCISM'

6

'Fascists', or 'Conservatives'?

The time has now come for us to look at some of the underlying characteristics of the movements that we have so far been observing, starting with the perennial problem of defining the terms 'conservative'* and 'radical', when applied to the Right.

It used to be the fashion to divide the various manifestations of the continental Right, in the inter-war period, into two fairly watertight categories. Movements could be classified either as 'fascist' or as 'conservative', according to whether their main lines of policy appeared to be either destructive or supportive of the status quo. Thus the French historian of the Right, René Rémond, found himself asking 'the fundamental question', in relation to each of the French extra-parliamentary movements he was studying: 'fascism or reaction?'. In the process, he came to the conclusion that there was 'no true French fascism'[1], as the most prominent movements – Action Française, Jeunesses Patriotes, Solidarité Française, Croix de Feu – were basically conservative and reactionary. The only exception he was prepared to make was for the Parti Populaire Français of Doriot. In opposition to such views, Zeev Sternhell, in his *Ni droite ni gauche*: *l'idéologie fasciste en France* (*Neither Right nor Left*: *the Fascist Ideology in France*) (1983), traced a major fascist influence in French thought and in French political movements of the same period, and linked it convincingly with the 'radical Right' traditions within pre-1914 France that he had so successfully charted in his previous book *La Droite révolutionnaire*: *les origines françaises du fascisme* (*The Revolutionary Right*: *the French origins of fascism*) (1978).

* English readers should not be misled into thinking that this term has anything to do with the English Conservative (with a capital 'C') tradition, which so often has stood for progressive change. It is, rather, a shorthand (with a lower case 'c') used to distinguish between two traditions of the continental Right.

Sternhell's intervention, however, did little to defuse the debate, which continued on the simplistic basis of categorising whole movements as either 'fascist' or 'conservative'. It took a remarkable collective volume, which appeared in 1990, to put the debate on a more subtle and at the same time more realistic footing. The title of this volume, *Fascists and Conservatives*, was at first sight unpromising; but its editor Martin Blinkhorn, in his introduction, showed just how far from the old monolithic characterisations his, and his contributors', approach was going to be:

> In cases such as those examined here, the definitions, typologies and taxonomies beloved of social scientists tend to fit uncomfortably the intractable realities which are the raw material of the historian. The more closely the data relating to the European right are scrutinized, the more lines stubbornly refuse to be drawn or, when drawn, to remain straight and motionless; exceptions disprove more rules than they prove; and all too rarely do the subjective and the objective coincide.[2]

While underlining the essentially different natures of 'conservatism' and of 'the radical Right', a number of the contributors to *Fascists and Conservatives* stressed the way in which these two entities intertwined within individual movements, to the extent that a precise classification of such movements in these terms becomes extremely difficult.

This approach is a fertile one for our present study. It will be useful to look at a few of the widely differing regimes which, with hindsight, have been dubbed 'conservative', or 'reactionary', as opposed to 'fascist'. We will concentrate in particular on the experience of Portugal, Spain and Hungary; in order to do so, we will need first to look once more at the French movement, Action Française, which had so much influence on Portugal in particular.

Action Française

We have already seen how influential, in other countries, Action Française was in the inter-war period. Portugal, Greece, Belgium, were merely a few of the countries in which an indigenous Right had been inspired by this French example. Was that example, and that influence, 'fascist', or 'conservative'? The question is a naïve one, but it is one that is often asked.

Action Française, like many movements on the 'radical Right', shared characteristics of both those strains of the Right that we have been considering. While harbouring traditional elements, it nevertheless had little in common with the French conservative tradition. Its pre-1914 emphasis on anti-capitalism was revolutionary, and 'fascistic'; but even its post-war partial conversion to capitalism would not have been out of place in fascism, for, as we have seen, in practice 'fascist' parties tended to feel the necessity to compromise with the forces of capitalism, and in particular with industrialists. The rhetoric of anti-capitalism remained, right up to the Second World War, part of the discourse of Action Française, whatever the movement's actual policies, and it was to find an echo in the radio speeches made by Marshal Pétain when Vichy took power in 1940. In them, under the influence of his Action Française advisers such as Raphaël Alibert and Henri Massis (who in great part wrote his speeches for him), he evoked the old virtues that had been destroyed by two materialisms, capitalism and communism.

The mixture of qualities that we find in Action Française stemmed in part from a conscious desire, on the part of Maurras, to appeal to as many constituencies as possible. An article of his, written in 1908, after referring to 'our Left, of which I am part', lists these constituencies, and the movement's responses to them:

Thus, to lead them to our cause [...] we have said to the patriots: 'if you really want to save your country ...'; to the nationalists: 'if you want to shake off the yoke of the foreigner in our midst ...'; to the anti-Semites: 'if you want to end the reign of the Jews ...'; to the conservatives: ' if the preservation of public order is stronger to you than your divisions, your prejudices, your prudence'; to the proletariat in heavy industry: 'if organisation of social forces seems to you more necessary than anything else ...'; and finally to the Catholics: 'if you wish to triumph over the persecutors of the Church ...'[3]

Most of those, in other countries, who came under the influence of Action Française, did so because it appeared to represent a *new* approach to the problems of the nation, and not because of any similarity to their indigenous nineteenth-century forms of reaction. The double character of Action Française makes it very difficult to classify. On the one hand, it stood for reasoned argument, and a rather fallacious 'intellectualism'; on the other there was its cult of violence, of street demonstrations and brawls. On the one hand it appeared the defender of the Church and of social order; on the other hand, its provenance from the 'revolutionary Right', its corporatist principles, its institutionalisation of violence, its use of the symbols of race and nation, and its revolutionary discourse, made it difficult to differentiate from the 'fascist' movements of the Thirties, even though certain characteristics (above all its monarchism) made it a fairly important variant of them.

As the Thirties wore on, it became even more difficult to differentiate between the attitudes of those who were firm adherents of Action Française, and those who saw themselves as participants in the new 'international fascism'. Action Française commentators, who in the Twenties had seen Italian Fascism as an interesting movement, comparable in certain respects to theirs (but no more than that), were beginning to see themselves as part of the new international experiment. Nowhere is this clearer than in the close relationship between Robert Brasillach of the *Je suis partout* group[4] (whom we have already seen as one of the greatest enthusiasts for 'international fascism') and Henri Massis, the pillar of Action Française. The two men shared a vision of 'Catholic fascism' which drew them to the Mediterranean manifestations of the new 'movement'; together they visited Spain in the course of the Civil War, and jointly they wrote two books devoted to it. In no way do they seem to have had any impression of a difference between their attitudes. In fact, their outlooks on political matters were almost identical.

Salazar's Portugal

That the Portuguese case is ambiguous is hardly surprising, given the strong influence of Action Française there. The most common definition given nowadays to Salazar's regime is 'conservative'; Rémond declares that Portugal under his rule could in no way be placed under the category 'fascist', and summarily dismisses it as 'a conservative, clerical regime'.[5] We must of course beware, when contradicting this, of attempting to substitute for it the equally simplistic generalisation 'fascist'. Rather, we here find the frontiers between the different Rights becoming blurred, even from our privileged position of hindsight; how much more so, when we examine the actual position at the time, and the perceptions held by the protagonists as to the nature of 'fascism' and 'conservatism'.

Observers have noted, in Portugal from the nineteenth century onwards, 'an intellectual and stylistic dependence on France', which culminated towards the end of the century with the influence of 'social catholicism and literary nationalism of the Barrès type'.[6] Shortly thereafter, Action Française 'found many disciples among both the Integralists and the Catholic intellectuals'. The Integralist movement, founded in 1914, based its doctrines on the French movement, and the Sidónio Pais dictatorship, in 1918, put into practice corporatist doctrines, under the influence of the Integralists.

After the Army coup of 28 May 1926, Salazar was brought in as Finance Minister in the government of General Gomes da Costa, but soon resigned because the government at first refused to implement his policies. In July 1928, however, he returned, and restored the health of the economy in the years 1928-1933, installing a form of corporatism. In 1932 he became Prime Minister, and in March 1933 the New State, the Estado Novo, was inaugurated, whereby Portugal became a corporative and unitary republic.

When speaking of the Salazar regime, people tend to make a distinction between Salazar the 'conservative' and the 'fascists' of the National Syndicalist party, which he suppressed in 1934. This distinction (and the myth of Salazar, like Maurras, being an intellectual who had wandered into politics),[7] is at the root of all the definitions of Salazar as a basically non-fascist conservative. But Salazarism and National Syndicalism had more in common than they had differences. Both owed much to the tradition of Integralism. And, as Martins underlines, Integralism was the breeding ground for the new 'fascism' of the inter-war period:

At the time when Italian fascist and Nazi models assumed 'world-historical' importance, those most disposed to learn from and emulate them had all been grounded in the teachings and intellectual style of *Integralismo*.[8]

The description Gallagher gives of Salazar shows the similarities between his ideas, at the beginning, and those of the Integralists:

Salazar [...] since his youth had been strongly influenced by Maurras. [...] Other influences were papal social doctrine and the writings of French conservative sociologists like Le Play.[9]

The leaders of the National Syndicalist movement had all been members of the Integralist movement from its beginnings. Although their movement was a more urgent manifestation of these ideas, it nevertheless remained a continuation of a revolutionary Right that was already existent in Portugal.

The only difference between Salazar and the National Syndicalists lay in tactics and not in doctrines. Both existed on the vague frontiers between the radical Right and conservatism. If, in the first years of his dictatorship, Salazar found it necessary to suppress the National Syndicalists, this was no doubt, like Hitler suppressing the SA in the same year, because, in order to maintain the support given to his regime by important sections of Portuguese society, he needed to distance himself from the most extreme manifestations of the Right to which he belonged.

Not that a parallel between Salazar and Hitler was valid on other grounds, particularly at this stage. For various reasons, Salazar was in 1934 distancing himself from the German and Italian dictators, and even from the concept of the 'totalitarian state' (at the very time when he was installing one).

However, the suppression of an internal extremist movement, and public criticism of the two most prominent foreign authoritarian regimes, tell us little about the nature of the Salazarian regime itself; and it is significant that, two years after his suppression of the National Syndicalists, two years after his denunciation of German- and Italian-style totalitarianism and 'absolutism', Salazar himself introduced in 1936 a whole series of measures of 'fascist' inspiration. Two new movements were founded: the *Mocidade Portuguesa* (a compulsory youth movement), and the Portuguese Legion, a para-military movement whose uniforms, 'Roman' salutes, and rhetoric, were all reminiscent of international fascism. At the same time, the activities of the PVDE (Policia de Vigilancia de Defesa do Estado), a secret police which existed for the suppression of all opposition, showed that, despite the rhetoric suggesting that it was a more liberal regime than the 'authoritarian' powers, Salazar's Estado Novo functioned as a police state.

Some commentators have traced the origin of these new developments to the beginning of the Spanish Civil War, and to the growing impression that Italian Fascism and German Nazism were becoming predominant in Europe, and worthy of emulation in face of the Bolshevik threat. As we have seen, there was much in the political activity of the mid and late Thirties which stemmed from contingent impressions, those myths which were becoming a reality. However, it must be admitted that there was nothing in these new developments (the Mocidade Portuguesa, the Portuguese legion, and the PVDE) which did not fit in with the basic principles that Salazarism had embodied from the beginning; and their creation, so soon after the suppression of the National Syndicalists, shows that that suppression had been a contingent event of political pragmatism rather than the expression of a doctrinal divergence.

Be that as it may, by the late Thirties, like so many other movements that had not until then seen themselves as owing anything to an Italian or German model, Salazarism began to conceive of itself as part of an 'international' pattern (and was also seen as such by contemporary observers). Despite his declarations at the beginning of the Thirties, Salazar appears by now to have seen his movement as being part of an 'Internationale' of authoritarian regimes, even though on certain questions such as the Anti-Comintern Pact he stood apart, maintaining a Portuguese independence. The neutrality of Portugal in the Second World War was another symptom of his prudence.

Paradoxically, the Portuguese experience tells us much about the profile of its model, Action Française. In an interview with Salazar in 1938, the Action Française enthusiast Henri Massis, hearing the principles of the Estado Novo, was moved to exclaim:

But these ideas are those propagated by the political
doctrine of Charles Maurras! In them are all de Maistre, all
La Tour du Pin, all Fustel de Coulanges, and also the teachings of the great Encyclicals! Yes, these ideas are ours; but
here we see them applied and realised by a man who
governs, incarnated in a real experience, inscribed in living
history. Their success proves to us that our ideas were not
abstractions, born of the 'esprit de système', but solid realities, from which a nation, before our eyes, is profiting in
order to be born again.[10]

By the late Thirties, as we have seen, for Action Française adher-
ents any differences that had formerly seemed apparent between
AF and 'fascism' were now subsumed in the new vibrant entity.
This impact of the new internationalism was to be found in
Salazar as well.

Franco's Spain

Unlike Salazar, Francisco Franco (1892-1975) had no previous
political 'form'. As a serving officer in the Spanish army he had
never expressed political views in public. His private views
appear to have been typical of the officer class of his time. They
have been described as follows:

His political views [...] were those of an *africanista*; a simple
nationalist and conservative, [...] who conceived of the military as the ultimate guarantor of national coherence, he had
little sympathy with parliamentary democracy.[11]

These opinions were shared by many on the Spanish Right.
Throughout the nineteenth and the early twentieth century, the
dominant force upon the Spanish Right had been what has been
described as 'Catholic traditionalism'. It had been the driving
force behind Carlism, which, though essentially a nineteenth-
century phenomenon, still had its place in the often
anachronistic politics of twentieth-century Spain; and it was to
be the basis for most movements of the Right in the twentieth
century.
Many of the elements which had militated for the emergence

of 'radical Right' politics in France, Italy and Germany were absent from the Spanish scene, which was something of a backwater in relation to developments in other parts of Europe. So it was that, when General Miguel Primo de Rivera (1870-1930) took power as dictator in September 1923, he did so as a support to the apparently tottering monarchy.

Primo de Rivera's dictatorship was in the direct line of those military interventions which had studded Spain's history. It had been set up, in nineteenth-century style, on the basis of a *pronunciamiento* by the General to the King (the forty-third since 1814!). However, once stability of government had been established, and the monarchy safeguarded, the regime appears above all to have been a mildly paternalistic one, with Primo starting various attempts at reform of Spain's legacy of social inequality. It has been suggested that it was these attempts that lost him the support of the traditional Right, and of the army itself; though the slump may also have affected his popularity. In 1930, deserted by those who had supported his accession, including his brother-officers, he retired, and died shortly thereafter.

The fall of Primo de Rivera was followed by the fall of the monarchy in 1931. The advent of the Republic led to disarray on the Right. Amazingly, one of the first effects was a resurgence of Carlism (the movement supporting the Restoration of the Carlist branch of the Spanish royal family), which since the 1830s had stood for anti-liberal extremism.

In the early years of the Second Republic there was little evidence of support for 'fascist' or 'radical Right' movements. Two such movements were formed, it is true, in the years 1931-3: *Juntas de Ofensiva Nacional Syndicalista* (JONS), founded in 1931, and the *Falange Española*, founded in October 1933 (whose leader was José Antonio Primo de Rivera, son of the former dictator). José Antonio (1903-1936) had, before forming the *Falange*, visited Mussolini; and the policies he developed for his movement were those of an 'anti-party of neither left nor right'[12], which was nevertheless rooted in Catholic nationalism. In 1934 the *Falange Española* and the JONS merged as the *Falange Española de las JONS*. But neither had had much success, at this stage, in attracting adherents; and, though the new joint party did expand its membership a little, there appeared to be little future for a 'fascist' movement in Spain. In the election of 1936 the Falange obtained only 0.7 per cent of the vote.

Though the Army showed little inclination to support any of the political movements here mentioned, there is no doubt that it saw its role as remaining that of ensuring an orderly state, which they would defend against all subversive forces (among which should now be counted Republicanism). As early as August 1932, General Sanjurjo produced yet another *pronunciamiento*; his rising, however, was disastrously unsuccessful. It was to be four years before another, more successful, military uprising was to cause possibly the most disastrous civil war in Spain's turbulent history.

Franco himself played no part in the events of 1932. He remained loyal to the Republic. In 1933 he was given the post of Captain General of the Balearic Islands. In 1934 he acted as adviser to the War Minister in putting down the rebel miners in the Asturias, and the insurgents in Catalonia. As a result, he was appointed Commander of the Spanish forces in Morocco in January 1935. Throughout this period people seem to have found it hard to know what his political attitude was.

Amid the mounting political unrest following on the brutal suppression by the Republic and its army of the Asturias miners' revolt and the Catalan rebellion in 1934, the success of a Popular Front alliance in the elections of February 1936 proved a catalyst. Violence and murder stalked the country in the succeeding months. Fearful of the undermining of the stability of Spanish society, the Right (including of course the Army) began to organise itself. A military conspiracy took shape, under Generals Mola and Sanjurjo. Franco himself had, at the advent of the Popular Front government, been removed from his post, and sent to the Canary Islands as Captain-General. Here he at first stayed aloof from the plot, but eventually realised, by July 1936, that he must join. Franco's role was to fly to Morocco to take command of the Army of Africa, which, after crossing the Straits, was to play a major part in the campaign in Spain itself. The rising began on the night of 17-18 July. Though the rebels' command originally consisted of a *junta* of generals, by the end of the year Franco was Generalissimo, and had been proclaimed Head of State.

It is easy to see why political observers in our own time have been led to categorise Franco, and his eventual regime, as 'conservative' rather than fascist. The attempted military coup appears to have been similar to many others in Spanish history. The *Falange*, it is true, was to play a considerable part in Nationalist activities, and its numbers were to grow immeasurably from the moment of the advent of the Popular Front Government, accelerating after the outbreak of the revolt, and rising to about 50,000. By the end of 1936, however, José Antonio Primo de Rivera had been executed, and most of the other prominent *Falange* leaders killed, and the vast new movement was resultantly politically weak. In April 1937 Franco, after arresting the Falangist leader Manuel Hedilla, pulled off the remarkable coup of incorporating (and, according to some, submerging) the *Falange* in vast new party containing all the parties that supported the Nationalists; by calling it the *Falange Española Tradicionalista y de la JONS*, he appeared to be linking the new movement with the traditions of the *Falange*; but he himself was to be the head of this new party.

The judgement of hindsight, therefore, classifies Franco and his regime as 'conservative' in essence; and the history of post-war Spain seems on the surface to justify this, particularly from the nineteen-fifties onwards. But one must nevertheless consider various factors which make the situation less clear as far as the Thirties and Forties are concerned. Firstly, the creation of a single State party was very much in line with 'fascist' procedures. Secondly, the *Falange*, despite its weakened status, still, as Paul Preston has pointed out, set 'the regime's ideological tone' after the Civil War and during the Second World War. Thirdly, Franco himself does not seem to have viewed the amalgamation of the Falange into the unitary party in the same way that some historians have. Speaking to the German ambassador of his plans, in April 1937, he is reported thus:

Regarding his attitude toward the Falange and the monarchist parties, Franco told me that he wished to fuse these groups into one party, the leadership of which he himself would assume. [...] The core of the unity party would be formed by the Falange, which had the soundest program and the greatest following in the country.

The German ambassador's judgement on the situation that might arise if there was a conflict between Franco and the Falange shows that he believed Franco's policies to be basically in line with fascism, whatever his relationship with that movement:

> If in his attempt to bring the parties together Franco should meet opposition from the Falange, we and the Italians are agreed that, in spite of all our inclination toward the Falange and its sound tendencies, we must support Franco, who after all intends to make the program of the Falange the basis of his internal policy.[13]

All this does not necessarily mean, of course, that Franco wholeheartedly espoused the more radical parts of fascist social theory. His Spanish Labour Charter, produced in 1938 was more paternalistic and regulatory than the 'fascist' model. And later, of course, the original aims of Falangism itself were to become diluted, to the extent that it 'lost any autonomous dynamism when, after the unification, it allowed itself to provide the bureaucratic structure of the new Francoist state':

> The Falange became the arena for place-seeking, the ever-flexible rhetoric of its leaders merely a means of currying favour and gaining promotion. The goal of national-syndicalist revolution was quietly dropped in the quest for the safe billets of state functionaries. Agrarian reform and the nationalisation of banks became part of the 'pending revolution'.[14]

In the period 1937-1945, however, there is little doubt that 'in the eyes of the outside world, the Falange and Francoism were consubstantial'. We have already seen the extent to which contemporary observers not only referred to the Nationalists as 'fascists', but also drew attention to the 'international' nature of the fascist threat as now seen in Spain. How wrong were they to do so?

However 'conservative' Franco and his military colleagues may have been, the atmosphere of the late Thirties was such that any authoritarian movement appeared to be part of 'international fascism'. And Germany and Italy both provided considerable material help to Franco's cause. Their reasons for this were of course mixed, and in large part due to self-interest: Mussolini's desire not to have a left-wing regime in Spain thwarting his Mediterranean ambitions, Germany's need for Spanish iron ore, Germany's need to divert the attention of the West from German rearmament – but the fact that Franco himself could confidently ask for such help, obviously feeling some affinity between these two regimes and his own cause, was significant. Within days of the outbreak of the war he sent emissaries to Rome to approach the Italian Government about the supply of war material. On 22 July he sent a request to the Germans for help in transporting his troops to Spain. Between 29 July and 5 August, German Junkers transport aircraft carried about half of Franco's Army of Africa to Seville, in a remarkable air lift which was instrumental in the initial successes of the Nationalist cause, while Italian fighters covered the merchant ships which ferried the other half of the Army to mainland Spain. This initial help was a mere foretaste of things to come. The German and Italian contribution to the Nationalist war effort was considerable.

What was Franco's own view of his position vis-à-vis 'international fascism'? As with so many of his contemporaries, he did not seem as clear about the terms he was using as later commentators were to be. By the later stages of the war he clearly, like so many others (both his supporters and his opponents), saw what had been happening in Spain as being part of an international trend. In a 1938 interview with the French writer Henri Massis, while insisting on the difference between his regime and the Hitlerian system, he spoke of several different manifestations of 'fascism', of which the Spanish unitary party was one:

Fascism, since that is the word that is used, fascism presents, wherever it manifests itself, characteristics which are varied to the extent that countries and national temperaments vary. It is essentially a defensive reaction of the organism, a manifestation of the desire to live, of the desire not to die, which at certain times seizes a whole people.

So each people reacts in its own way, according to its conception of life. Our rising, here, has a Spanish meaning! What can it have in common with Hitlerism, which was, above all, a reaction against the state of things created by the defeat, and by the abdication and the despair that followed it?[15]

Thus, while differentiating between several 'fascisms', Franco characterised his own movement as being fascist 'since that is the word that is used'. But, as the interview proceeded, a further complication arose, caused by the fact that the word 'fascist' could have two meanings: an international political tendency, and a specific Italian movement which had invented the name. (As we have seen, in English the ambiguity is solved by the use of a capital 'F' for the actual Italian movement, but in French, the language in which Massis reported this interview, the distinction was less clear). Franco had initially used the word in the first sense; but, while trying to stress the 'Spanish' and national character of his own movement, he differentiated it, too, from the Italian movement; in the process, he used the word in the purely Italian sense: 'Our movement', he said, 'does not run the risk of being subjected to a foreign deformation [...] It does not run the danger of "Fascising" itself, even less of "Nazifying" itself'.

So there are these two possible meanings of the word 'fascism' on one single page of Massis's interview with Franco! For Franco, definitions do not seem to have been of much importance. What he stressed in this interview, nevertheless, was that he saw the Spanish movement as being related to the rise of dictatorial regimes of the Right throughout Europe, regimes which displayed many differences from each other but which had this in common: that they were a reaction against the dangers of the Left and of political chaos, that they had a 'desire to live', that they were based upon the will of a people. These regimes, 'since that is the word that is used', were all 'fascist'.

Other statements by Franco, in this period, give the same impression of acceptance of a 'fascist' label. Outlining, for example, in a speech to his forces in April 1937, the history of the Spanish Right which had led to the present moment, he described the regime of Primo de Rivera as having been 'a period of transition between the Pronunciamiento of the nineteenth century and the organic conception of those movements that our present-day world labels 'fascist' or 'nationalist'.[16]

And, just as their opponents readily saw the Spanish

Nationalists as 'fascists', so the devotees of the new creed of 'international fascism' perceived the Spanish experience as being the testing-ground of the new faith. As Robert Brasillach, at the end of an enumeration of all the different types of European fascism, wrote:

> Finally, at a time when all the diverse doctrines were either still waiting for power, or had seized it without an extended battle (even German national socialism), a terrible struggle broke out in one of the most noble lands of Europe, and opposed *fascism* and *antifascism* to each other in bloody combat. Spain thus succeeded in transforming the long opposition that had been smouldering in the modern world, into a combat that was both spiritual and material, a true crusade. [...] In the grey smoke of the shells, under the blazing sky criss-crossed by fighter planes, Russians against Italians, the ideological contradictions were resolved, in this ancient land of acts of faith and of conquest, by suffering, by blood, by death. Spain gave its consecration, and a definitive nobility, to the war of ideas.[17]

Horthy's Hungary[18]

Admiral Miklós von Horthy, the Regent of Hungary from 1920 to 1945, presents very different problems. For the greater part of his rule, particularly in the Twenties and early Thirties, he and his regime appeared unmistakably 'conservative' in a way that neither Salazar nor Franco were. In this sense, he would appear a touchstone for our examination of other movements; a 'non-fascist' example alongside which to put the more ambiguous regimes we have been examining. Yet the later Thirties and the wartime experience of Hungary brought new features that some might take to modify this view.

Miklós von Horthy was an admiral, who by the end of the war had become commander-in-chief of the Austro-Hungarian fleet (which was based In Trieste on the Adriatic). He came to power in 1920 as a popular restorer of some kind of status quo, after Hungary's bitter experiences of the preceding two years. At the end of the First World War, amid popular demonstrations, King

Karl IV (King of Hungary and Emperor of Austria) had abdicated on 13 November 1918, and on 16 November the 'People's Republic of Hungary' had been proclaimed, initially under the Presidency of Count Mihály Károlyi. Hungary's post-war situation was soon seen to be a desperate one. Added to the loss of morale of a nation that had been on the losing side, it was also clear that a large part of pre-war Hungary (in the event over 70%) was to be lost to Romania and to the two new Slavonic nations Czechoslovakia and Yugoslavia, and that as a result of that loss the national economy would scarcely be viable. Amid mounting chaos, the Socialists allied themselves with the Communists (whose leader was Béla Kun), the new party being called 'the Socialist Party of Hungary'. On 21 March 1919 Károlyi ceded power to these forces, and a Soviet Republic was created.

This regime was a doctrinaire Marxist one, in which all businesses and banks were expropriated, and trade declared a state monopoly. In the countryside, terrorist forces committed murder and mayhem. Almost all sections of society were alienated by the regime's activities. Counterrevolutionary forces began to organise themselves in outlying areas, particularly in the Southeast, and when, in July 1919, the Romanian army invaded in order to topple the regime, they received much support. On 1 August Béla Kun and his commissars fled; a few days later the Romanians occupied Budapest. A counterrevolutionary government and army, under Admiral Horthy, which had been formed in Szeged during the Bolshevik rule, was unable at this stage to come to Budapest because of the Romanian occupation.

After the departure of the Romanians, Horthy and his army entered Budapest. Elections held in January 1920 returned a heavily conservative majority. Hungary was declared a kingdom, and Horthy was elected Regent in March. The decision to remain a kingdom was in large part a reaction against the short-lived republic under Károlyi, which was seen as having provided the platform from which the Bolshevik takeover had been possible. Most Hungarians, however, had no desire for a return of the Habsburgs, and when in 1921 ex-King Karl IV tried on two occasions to lay claim to the throne, Horthy opposed him, in April by peaceful means, in October by force of arms. The Hungarian Government then legislated for the official dethronement of the

Habsburg dynasty, and from 1921 onwards Horthy was a regent without a king (as well as being an admiral without a navy, in a landlocked country).

Horthy was from now on in the position of a dictator. He chose the Prime Minister, convened and dissolved parliament, and there was no way in which he could be called to account. He was also Supreme Commander of the Army, which was under his direct command. What we must bear in mind is that this position made him responsible for any actions undertaken by the regime (which would appear to invalidate some of the justifications for Horthy undertaken by cold-war historians after the Second World War).

The stability of Horthy's regime rested on a number of factors. Firstly, he was genuinely popular with a large section of the community; secondly, there was a tradition of authoritarian government in Hungary, and the Károlyi experiment had warned people of the dangers of democracy; thirdly, the experience of the Béla Kun regime had shown, it was believed, the need for firm government; fourthly, the territorial losses as a result of the peace treaty evoked a national mood of 'revanchism' which a military dictatorship did much to reassure.

Horthy's regime was marked to a significant extent by anti-Semitism. As we have seen, anti-Semitism does not necessarily denote 'fascism'. It was endemic in Eastern Europe (and particularly strong, for example, in Poland). Though Hungary's nineteenth-century history had given evidence of considerable liberalism in the treatment of Jews, anti-Semitism had never been far from the surface; and the fact that the Béla Kun government had consisted in large part of Jews now provided the fuel to stoke the fires of race hatred. In the nineteen-twenties, under the conservative prime minister Count István Bethlen, this anti-Semitism was not translated into measures of any significance; but by the late Thirties the picture was to be different.

In the Thirties, after the Nazis took power in Germany, Hungary could not ignore its powerful neighbour. Indeed, in the ever-keen pursuit of restoration of the 'lost lands', some saw considerable advantage in a German alliance, though others feared German expansion. Under Prime Minister Gyula Gömbös (1932-6) the country took on a more German orientation, in the hope of a division of spoils in Central Europe. Gradually,

Hungary moved towards becoming a German satellite. This was to pay off, with successive gains of territory from 1938 to 1941.

It has been argued that all this should not necessarily be taken to mean that Hungary had become 'fascist'. The alliance with Germany was, it is said, governed by Hungary's foreign policy imperatives, and not by a sympathy for Germany's governing ideology. The fact that there *were*, from the early Thirties onwards, movements within Hungary which imitated the German model, but that they were systematically suppressed under the authoritarian regime of Horthy, has been cited as further proof of the 'non-fascist' nature of the regime.

Contemporary views produce a rather different picture. To many, whether fascist or anti-fascist, Hungary's increasing dependence on Germany in the Thirties seemed, in the spirit of the new idea of 'international fascism', to classify the Horthy regime as one further part of that international movement; and the anti-Semitic laws of 1938 and 1939 appeared to confirm this view. The post-war 1950 *Encyclopaedia Britannica* continued to hold to this standpoint:

> With the Gömbös ministry Hungary entered a period of progressive fascistization [sic] of its whole life. Close co-operation with Fascist Italy and, after Hitler's accession to power, with national socialist Germany, became the guiding principle of Hungary's foreign policy.

After Gömbös's death in 1936 there was a short period of indecision, but in 1938 the die was finally cast, as Hungary became even more closely associated with Germany. This coincided with anti-Semitic legislation which restricted the participation of Jews in Hungary's political and economic life. Swiftly Hungary's position became more entrenched. In November 1938 she shared in the eventual spoils of the Munich agreement. Then she left the League of Nations. Soon, further anti-Semitic legislation was passed. In March 1939 she shared once more in the spoils of the former Czechoslovakia. In February 1939 the otherwise pro-German Premier Imrédy was forced to resign (with Horthy's approval) because he was found to be partly of Jewish descent. In May 1939 further drastic anti-Semitic laws were passed.

Admittedly, Horthy's successive governments had on the

whole suppressed internal 'fascist movements'. After Hitler's accession to power, many little Hungarian movements had copied Nazi policies and symbols more or less slavishly. None of them had come to anything very much, however, particularly as they were continually at warfare with each other. Ferenc Szálasi (1897-1946) had however been a very different matter. In 1935 this former army officer founded a movement called the Party of the National Will, which began to pose more of a threat. By 1937 (the year in which Szálasi was arrested and sentenced to three months' prison), now called the Arrow Cross, and promoting a doctrine of national socialism, it had grown to about 20,000 members.

By 1938, Szálasi's party was being funded by the Germans, and was able to buy the support of a section of the press. After rumours of the preparation of a coup, Szálasi was arrested, and sentenced to three years' hard labour. Though the Arrow Cross movement was harassed thereafter by mass imprisonments, and by a ban on its meetings and its newspapers, it gained popular support to the extent that it and its allies gained 49 seats in the elections of May 1939.

Szálasi was released from prison in 1940, but his movement continued to be kept on the fringes of national life, repressed by the Horthy regime, whose popularity had been enhanced by the territorial gains that its foreign policy had given the country. Horthy's repression of Szálasi's movement was not necessarily based on 'anti-fascism' (which has sometimes been ascribed to it), so much as the natural desire by a dictatorship to suppress opposition parties that appeared to be gaining public support, and which were severely critical of the regime.

At the outbreak of the Second World War in 1939, Hungary had at first remained neutral, while stressing her sympathy with Germany, a sympathy which paid off with the annexation of northern Transylvania from Romania to Hungary in August 1940. Two months later, Hungary signed the Axis Pact. Further anti-Jewish legislation was enacted. In 1941 Hungary entered the war as an ally of Germany.

Horthy's attitude, as the war progressed, was an equivocal one, aimed at ensuring Hungary's future, whichever of the belligerents finally won. From March 1942 onwards, with a new Prime Minister, Miklós Kállay, he pursued a policy of preparing

Hungary's defences against the Soviets, and at the same time preparing to work with the Allies, if they were victorious, in keeping the Russians out of Western Europe. In internal policies, in the years 1942-44, the Horthy regime, further to its anti-Semitic laws of 1938-40 and in accordance with its underlying anti-Semitism, enacted various further serious measures against the Jews, including Labour Camps. But, as an ally of Germany, and not an occupied country, Hungary did not participate at this stage in the 'Final Solution' (possibly because of Horthy's concerns about relations with the Allies if they won the war).

In March 1944 the Russian advance brought them close to Hungary. Horthy was at this stage summoned to a meeting with Hitler, and threatened, if he came to terms with the western Allies, with an attack on Hungary by Germany and her allies Romania, Slovakia and Croatia. He was forced to allow the German army to enter Hungary (which they did on 19 March), and to appoint a new pro-German Prime Minister, General Döme Sztójay. Under this new regime of Horthy's the fate of the Jews was transformed, firstly by even more severe restrictions on their activities, and, eventually, from May onwards, by deportation as part of the Final Solution, under the direction of Eichmann himself. By July almost half a million Jews had been removed from Hungary and deported to extermination camps.

It is reasonable to suppose that Horthy was not particularly concerned by this. His anti-Semitic credentials had been shown from the Thirties onwards; and, though he would certainly not have participated in the Final Solution without Hitler's forceful intervention, any qualms he may have had would almost certainly have been based on a concern to placate the Allies. The first international protests (including one from the Vatican) did not have too much effect. But a telegram from Roosevelt on 25 June was a different matter. In it, Roosevelt threatened dire results for Hungary; the bombing of Budapest, and due punishment after the Allied victory. In July, as a result of Roosevelt's intervention, Horthy stopped the deportations and dismissed Sztójay, whose successor was ordered to start negotiations for an armistice with the Russians, who by now were on Hungarian soil.

Amid all this, the egregious Szálasi emerged once more upon the scene. He offered his services to the Germans, and, on 15

October, the day that Horthy publicly announced the armistice with the Russians, the Germans arrested Horthy and imposed Szálasi as Prime Minister. In the two months before the Red Army surrounded Budapest, severe repression of the Jews was reinstituted. However, by December the collaborators were forced to flee, first to eastern Hungary, and then to exile in Germany. A new Government in Budapest made peace with the Russians, and declared war on Germany.

For most of its early existence, Horthy's regime was probably the most pure example of the 'conservative' Right that one could find in inter-war Europe. And though, by the nature of Hungary's interests, Horthy was pro-German for most of the late Thirties, this does not imply any 'national socialist' element in his political philosophy. Hungary's physical closeness to the 'Greater Germany' of which from 1938 onwards Austria was a part, meant that it was materially called to an alliance, and to become a part of the 'New Order'.

The Horthy regime's anti-Semitism, however, brought it closer to Nazism in another way; the extermination policies of mid-1944, though imposed by Germany, were in no way alien to the regime's prejudices. Horthy's close association with Nazi Germany from the late Thirties onwards, and his active participation in the Final Solution in 1944, show that this 'conservative' could ally himself with 'fascist' policies in a way that makes him an ambiguous figure in the 'conservative-fascist' debate.

For those for whom the word 'fascist', in its more simplistic post-war definition, means above all authoritarianism and anti-Semitism, Horthy can easily be classified as a 'fascist'. If we compare him with the inter-war regimes that were clearly 'fascist', however, all is not so clear, as he shared few of the other characteristics we would associate with fascism. To contemporaries in the climate of the late Thirties, however, his conservative regime had become as much a part of 'international fascism' as those of Salazar, of Franco, of Codreanu, or of any of the other myriad movements and dictatorships spawned in the inter-war period. Even Horthy, therefore, presents an element of ambiguity in our study.

*

112   *An Intelligent Person's Guide to Fascism*

In the debate about 'fascism' and 'conservatism', we have seen that Horthy's Hungary stands as a deceptively straightforward case. As in almost every other situation where movements of the Right in inter-war Europe are classified by modern scholars as 'conservative', the situation is far more complicated than it has been made to seem. The regimes of the 'conservatives' Salazar and Franco contained, in varying degrees, characteristics both of the 'radical Right' and of the 'reactionary Right'; and, as the Thirties progressed, and 'international fascism' became an accepted concept, the association of their movements with 'fascism', both by opponents and by supporters, became very much the norm. Horthy was, in his internal policies, far more straightforwardly 'conservative' than either Salazar or Franco; but his close alliance with Nazi Germany makes even his position in some respects an ambiguous one. Nothing could illustrate more clearly the ultimate futility of trying to produce hard-and-fast distinctions between 'fascist' and 'conservative' movements and regimes in the Thirties.

1. René Rémond, *La Droite en France de la Première Restauration à la Ve. République*, Aubier 1963, p. 221.
2. Martin Blinkhorn, Introduction to *Fascists and Conservatives*, London, Unwin Hyman 1990, pp. 1-2.
3. Charles Maurras, 'Réponses au Correspondant', in *L'Action Française. Revue Bi-mensuelle*, 1 Feb. 1908, pp. 242, 255.
4. Described as 'the major vehicle for literary fascism in France in the Thirties'.
5. Rémond, op.cit., p. 214.
6. H. Martins, 'Portugal', in *European Fascism*, ed. S.J. Woolf, London, Weidenfeld and Nicolson, 1968, p. 303.
7. The researches of Professor Manuel Cabral have shown just how active Salazar's political plans had been well before his call to government (contrary to the myth of the 'reluctant professor' being dragged into power).
8. Martins, op. cit., p. 304.
9. Tom Gallagher, 'Conservatism, dictatorship and fascism in Portugal, 1914-45', in Martin Blinkhorn (ed.), *Fascists and Conservatives*, London, Unwin Hyman, 1990, p. 158.
10. Henri Massis, *Chefs*, Paris, Plon, 1939, p. 94.
11. Philip Rees, *Biographical Dictionary of the Extreme Right since 1890*, Harvester Wheatsheaf 1990, p. 132.
12. Rees, op.cit., p. 304.
13. Report of German ambassador, 14 April 1937, quoted in Charles F. Delzell (ed.), *Mediterranean Fascism 1919-1945*, Harper and Row 1970, p. 288.
14. Paul Preston, 'Populism and parasitism: the Falange and the Spanish establishment 1939-75', in *Fascists and Conservatives*, p. 140.
15. Henri Massis, *Chefs*, Paris, Plon, 1939, p. 150.

16. Franco's Call for the Unification of the Fighting Forces, 18 April 1937, quoted in Delzell, op.cit., p. 288.

17. Robert Brasillach, *Notre Avant-guerre*, p. 305.

18. For much of the historical information in this section, I am indebted to István Deák's chapter 'Hungary' in Rogger and Weber, *The European Right*, pp. 364-407.

Two Variants of the 'International Fascism' of the Late Thirties

'Catholic Fascism' and the 'Iron Guard'

By the late Thirties, both Left and Right were agreed about one thing: whatever the apparent differences between the various movements and regimes concerned, there was now such a thing as 'international fascism'. In the words of Sir Oswald Mosley: 'The universalism of Fascism and National Socialism erects the majestic edifice of a new world idea which commands the mind and spirit of man with the fiery force of a new religion'.[1] It was stressed, of course, that the movements and regimes concerned were in no way identical to each other. As nationalism was one of the main things that they had in common, that nationalism was bound to have different characteristics in each country. As Franco said, 'Fascism presents, wherever it manifests itself, characteristics which are varied to the extent that countries and national temperaments vary'.[2] Yet fascism, despite this great variety, was seen as an entity (even if not everyone went as far as the English Catholic commentator James Strachey Barnes had gone, in comparing the diversity yet unity of fascism to the Trinity, one God in three Persons).

In this new way of looking at things, the various forms of fascist ideology, and their differences, were less important than the things that 'fascism' was reacting against, and than the outward impression given by the movements, their 'impact', their 'myths', their 'poetry'.

Fascism, it was generally agreed by its supporters, was a reaction against the 'decadence' of European society, and the 'despair' into which so many nations had fallen. In the aftermath of the First World War, society had spent its strength 'pursuing pointless goals on the margins of real events'. Fascism was 'the life-asserting reaction of a social body on the verge of exhaustion, and responding through those parts of it that are still healthy, to the effects of a slow intoxication'.[3] It was seen as a reaction, too, both to the materialism of western society and to the threat posed by international communism, a truly 'Third Way' which was the only solution to the ills of modern society. At the same time, racism, and the hatred of minorities, had become the ever-increasing down-side to this general picture (as the success of Nazism made it the central model for the new universal 'fascism').

So, according to their supporters, the various 'fascist' movements shared these negative hatreds, and shared a common purpose in attempting to put these things right. But they also shared a common emotional enthusiasm, based on 'myths' similar to those which Sorel had so graphically described:

It is of little importance to know what details, within myths, are destined to appear as dry facts upon the record of future history [...] We must judge myths as means of influencing the present.[4]

Among the fascist myths we must count not merely the ceremonies, the processions, the images from a national past, the uniforms, the salutes; there were also other emotive themes that perpetually recurred, across Europe: fitness, youth, comradeship, heroism. The French fascist author Robert Brasillach summed up most of this atmosphere in highly emotive terms:

The adversaries of fascism are completely unaware of the joy of fascism. Joy that you can criticise, or declare to be abominable or infernal, if that is your line, but JOY. The young fascist, backed up by his race and by his nation, proud of his vigorous body and of his lucid mind, despising the material goods of this world, the young fascist in his camp, amid comrades of peacetime who may become comrades of war, the young fascist as he sings, marches, works, dreams, he is above all a joyful being. [...] I do not know whether, as Mussolini has said, 'the twentieth century will be the century of fascism', but I know that nothing will prevent fascist joy from having existed, and from having inspired people's minds and souls by emotion and by reason.[5]

Not all the observers, even the sympathetic ones, would have followed Brasillach in his vision of the 'poetry' of fascism; but his enthusiastic vision does witness to the extent to which fascism was by now, to many of its supporters, an emotional experience rather than a coherent series of doctrines. Describing a car journey he had had, through the night, with the young Rexist leader Léon Degrelle, Brasillach wrote:

> I know that I will never forget that journey through the night, and the magic words which came from a young man faced with his destiny. I am sure that there can be no successful leader who is not imbued with a profound poetry. When he speaks to the Italians about their native land and their lands across the seas, Mussolini is a great poet, a descendant of the Latin poets of old, he evokes eternal Rome, and galleys on the *Mare nostrum*; and he is a poet, too, this Hitler who invents Walpurgis nights and May festivals, who mingles in his songs the Romanticism of the Cyclops and the Romanticism of the 'blue flower', the forest, the Venusberg, young girls gathering berries in the countryside and engaged to lieutenants in tank regiments, the comrades who fell in Munich in front of the Feldherrnhalle; and he is a poet, too, the Romanian Codreanu with his Legion of the Archangel Michael. There is no politics that is not made up of its share of images, there is no successful politics that is not *visible*.[6]

An 'over the top' vision! But, extreme as it is, this is a 'literary' reflection of the essentially non-ideological nature of so much support for fascism in the late Thirties, the emotional response of ordinary people to myths that seemed to take them out of their normally mundane existence, and the 'taking of sides' in a polarised battle between two forces. For many of these people, it was the 'virile' image of fascism, as opposed to the 'feminine' decadence of the age, which gave it its character. As Drieu la Rochelle, in a Sorellian celebration of conflict as opposed to peace, put it:

Fascism is the tension of European man, filled with the idea of a virile virtue that he feels to be threatened by the inevitable progress towards a definitive peace.[7]

All these diverse forms of myth coalesced into the central myth of international fascism itself. And if 'fascist' supporters were convinced of the universality of their creed, their opponents were of course even more clear in their minds about it, as they assessed the universal threat provided by the various movements of the Right throughout Europe. Given these contemporary views, we must accept the truth of these perceptions; and it is interesting to note the way in which movements that had previously been diverse began, in this period, to adopt the shared characteristics of the new creed. A great deal of diversity, however, nevertheless remained; and in this chapter we will be looking at two major variants of 'international fascism', which, though fundamentally different from each other, both found their basis in religion: 'Catholic fascism', and the Romanian Iron Guard.

'Catholic fascism'

There are a number of movements and regimes that would seem to fall under the definition of 'Catholic fascism' in the late Thirties: Franco's unitary party, Salazar's Estado Novo, Belgium's Rexism, Ireland's 'Blueshirts' and 'Greenshirts', and even (in some interpretations) Mussolini's Italy.

In Catholic circles abroad, views were mixed on Italy. Mussolini's signing of the Lateran Accords was, in some circles, hailed as a sign of the 'Catholic' nature of the regime. Professor Walter Starkie of the National University in Dublin, for example, claimed in 1938 that Mussolini had 'manifested on many occasions the deep reverence of his Government towards religion'.[8] Sir Charles Petrie, on the other hand, despite his great admiration for the Italian experiment, was not so blindly euphoric on this point as many other English Catholics. He realised that Mussolini was, and always would be, basically anti-clerical, as were many of his followers, and that the problem, for Mussolini, had been a purely political one. 'Both for Fascism and for Italy the backing of the Church would be invaluable if it could be secured on reasonable terms', he wrote.[9] What we have seen of Mussolini's career[10] would make one incline to this second, more cynical interpretation: that Mussolini realised the need for traditional Catholic support, and abandoned his overt anti-clericalism in order to work more closely with the Vatican, as part of the series of 'accommodations' that had moderated Fascist policies in order to mollify powerful constituencies. Despite this, it is important, however, to bear in mind the *impression* given, that all three dictatorships in the western Mediterranean were linked by their Catholicism.

This was particularly the impression given by the Nationalists in Spain. Much of the appeal of the Nationalist side, to Catholic observers from other countries, had been the rhetoric of the 'crusade' against anti-Christian forces. As one British enthusiast wrote in his diary on 26 January 1939:

> Got the glorious news about 2 p.m. that the Carlists had occupied Barcelona! Viva Réquétés! And so God in his infinite goodness has caused His Son to triumph again in Spain to the confusion and ruin of Red Anti-Christ. Viva Franco! Arriba España!

Foreign fascists saw this 'crusade' as presaging the arrival of a new 'Catholic fascism'. As Robert Brasillach put it:

> One can see how this Christian, fraternal spirit is far from that of National Socialism, of which we are nevertheless bound to admire the practical realisations. Spain may astonish the universe, if she so wishes – even more than Portugal – by installing a kind of fascist Catholicism [...] It is the sense of fraternity, of the communion of the faithful in the nation and in love, which serves as an active philosophy for this resurgent nation. And what amazes one is to see how swiftly this feeling has graduated from the level of doctrine to that of action.[11]

In the late Thirties, the close combination of Catholicism and 'fascism' seemed the norm in predominantly Catholic countries such as Spain and Portugal, or in those countries, such as Belgium, with a strong Catholic community. It is not surprising that one of the major influences upon such movements should have been, in the first instance, Action Française (even if later, in the climate of 'international fascism', the movements concerned forged affinities with the German and Italian experiments).

The 'fascist' movement of the French-speaking Belgians is a case in point. Its founder, Léon Degrelle (1906-95), was a product of the widespread enthusiasm for Maurras and the Action Française movement in the Belgium of the Twenties. Maurras's ideas and his rhetoric continued to be the basis of much Right-wing Catholic thought in Belgium, even after the Papal condemnation in 1926. Degrelle was educated at a Jesuit college in Namur and then at the Catholic University of Louvain, which he left in 1927. His early political influences were Léon Daudet and Charles Maurras, and he also read with admiration the writings of two French Catholic gurus: the right-wing soldier-philosopher Ernest Psichari, and the 'neither Right nor Left' friend of Georges Sorel, Charles Péguy. He soon became a protégé of Mgr Louis Picard, director of the movement 'Catholic Action of Belgian Youth' (*Action Catholique de la Jeunesse Belge*, or *ACJB*), and in 1929 he was made editor of its paper *Cahiers de la Jeunesse Catholique*. In 1930 Mgr Picard put him in charge of the publishing house Éditions Rex (a name based on Christ's title of 'Christus Rex', Christ the King). In 1932 Degrelle launched the journal *Rex*. This was used as the vehicle for more and more violent attacks, in Action Française mode, on high finance, freemasonry, communism, spiritual degeneracy, and politicians.

Degrelle, scornful of the complacent Catholic leadership in Belgium, founded the Rexist movement in early 1936, under what he claimed to be a new, youthful, dynamic leadership. Within six months the new movement had enormous success in the May 1936 elections, with 270,000 votes and 21 seats.

The policies of Rexism, at this stage, were very much in line with traditional Action Française ones – anti-capitalism, anti-communism, the importance of the family, the rejection of 'power élites', the sniffing-out of 'parliamentary corruption', and so on. The movement itself depended very much upon the image of its leader, his youth, energy, brilliant oratory and charisma. Indeed, soon the term 'Rex-appeal' made its appearance. Impressionable observers from other countries, such as Robert Brasillach, began to see Degrelle as the figurehead of a new fascist surge.

Soon, however, owing to a variety of factors, Rex began to lose its appeal. The voters turned back from it to more established parties. Degrelle had for some time been receiving subsidies from Mussolini. Now, impressed by Hitler (whom he had met at the time of the 1936 Olympics), he developed links with National Socialism.

By the 1939 elections the Rexist movement had ceased to be a power in the land. In May 1940 Degrelle was arrested as a Nazi sympathiser. Under the Occupation, he was released in July 1940. He soon became a fervent proponent of the case for Belgium becoming part of the Greater German Reich. In 1941 he formed the 'Légion Wallonie', one of the many military formations, in the occupied countries, which were created to fight alongside the Germans on the Russian front. He himself enlisted and fought in Russia, becoming the most decorated of the foreign members of the Waffen SS, as Sturmbannführer of the 3rd Brigade of the SS Division 'Wallonie'. At the end of the war, under condemnation of death, he escaped to Spain.

Rexism, then, is a very good example of the way in which, in the late Thirties, certain 'fascist' movements that had originally come from Catholic sources such as Action Française speedily took on the character of 'fellow travellers' of the Third Reich.

Elements of 'Catholic fascism' were to be found in most countries with a Catholic majority, even when the 'fascist' movements concerned were small and ineffective. Ireland is a case in point. As early as 1928 Professor Walter Starkie had been linking the idea of a 'spiritual awakening' for Ireland with the assimilation of 'a great deal of Fascist political doctrine, properly understood'. That he saw fascism as a religious force is shown by his declaration that only in this way could one avoid 'that selfish individualism and agnosticism which have formed the basis of political theory in modern times'.[12] In the early nineteen-thirties, Eoin O'Duffy's Blueshirts translated this into action. O'Duffy declared that the first function of the Blueshirts was 'to lead the Nation out of its present difficulties, and to set up the only Christian system of government which will work successfully in the modern world'. This system was corporatism. But 'for the Blueshirts themselves the setting up of an Irish Corporative State will not mark the final achievement; it will indeed be no more than the beginning of our work'. What was the main work to be? The renewal of Ireland as a Christian state, and the defence against communism and materialism:

> Our main work will always be to inspire our people with a consciousness of the great destiny of Ireland as a Christian State, and to promote in the coming generations the spirit which sent and is still sending Irish missionaries to the very ends of the earth. When the chaos of the dark ages broke over Europe, Irishmen saved Christianity even in Italy itself, and we should never forget that our proudest traditions are cultural and Christian. Chaos seems again to be about to spread all over the world; let us resolve that once again Ireland, the last outpost of Europe, will be ready to relive her historic past and stem the tide of Communism and materialism.[13]

The characteristics of the Blueshirts – corporatism, uniforms and fascist salutes, anti-democratic principles, etc., all show the movement to have been related to the other movements in the Thirties that we have been examining; and the fact that its corporatism was more in line with the Portuguese model than the Italian (being based on Catholic social theory, and similar to Action Française teachings) is a further link with many of these others. O'Duffy and his most prominent followers showed great admiration for Mussolini, and for the successes of Italian Fascism and of Nazism. The Blueshirts, however, had from 1933 (when their name became the League of Youth) been incorporated in a new party, the Fine Gael, many of whose policies were less 'fascistic'. Pressure from within this movement led to O'Duffy resigning from it in 1934, and in June 1935 he founded the National Corporate Party, known as 'the Greenshirts'. He forged closer links with 'international fascism', and like Codreanu's henchman Mota, took part in efforts to forge a 'fascist international'. And, again like the Romanians, he formed a brigade to fight in Spain for Franco. When he came back from Spain in June 1937, however, he gave up politics.

The O'Duffy experiments, though among the least successful of the movements we have been examining, were similar in kind to most of the other manifestations of 'Catholic fascism', in that they combined the corporative principles common to fascism, to

Action Française and to Catholic social policy, with the trappings of the totalitarian, anti-democratic movements of the period; and in that they also *perceived* themselves, by the mid and late Thirties, as being part of the 'fascist international' so many of whose characteristics they shared.

The Romanian 'Iron Guard'

Though ostensibly based on Christian principles, the 'Iron Guard' differs fundamentally from 'Catholic fascism' through its almost pagan elements (despite its Orthodox basis), and through the viciousness of its East European obsession with the Jews. It is also one of the best examples we have of a movement, originally entirely unconnected with 'fascism', which in the Thirties became regarded as a major example of that movement.

Corneliu Codreanu (1899-1938) was a product of the religious education given at Romanian military schools; he learned, in the words of Eugen Weber, 'respect for order and discipline, hierarchy and honour, "fear of God and only of God" '.[14] After the First World War, there were general Romanian fears of Bolshevik revolution of the kind Hungary was undergoing, and this, coupled with the anti-Semitism shared by so many of the Romanian people, was to be the basis for his political activity. In 1923, he founded with Alexandre Cuza the League of National Christian Defence, whose policy was mainly anti-Semitic. In October of that year Codreanu was arrested for conspiracy to murder a number of politicians who had voted for a measure to emancipate Jews. Though eventually acquitted, Codreanu had an extraordinary experience in prison: in some accounts he had a vision of the Archangel Michael, in others he was mystically influenced by an image of that Archangel in the chapel of the prison. Both versions agree that he felt himself to be urged to found a movement dedicated to Christian action. This movement, originally called the Brothers of the Cross, became in June 1927 the Legion of the Archangel Michael. It centred around elaborate rites of initiation, and its beliefs were based in a Manichean vision of the world being a battleground between the light and the dark, the forces of good and the forces of evil.

The Legion's main policies were anti-Semitic and anti-foreigner (in particular, the Bulgarian, Greek and Hungarian minorities). In 1930 a paramilitary formation of the Legion was founded under the name of the Iron Guard; soon, this became a title used for the movement as a whole.

Throughout the Thirties, the movement gained in power and in support; and, in the atmosphere of the times, it began to see itself as not purely a Romanian nationalist movement, but as part of 'international fascism' – despite the fact that none of its social policies had had much to do with those of the 'radical Right'. Admiration was expressed for the two 'fascist' governments that dominated the European scene, Nazism and Italian Fascism. As early as 1934 Codreanu's right-hand man, Ion Mota, represented the movement at the Fascist International in Montreux. During the Spanish Civil War, the Romanians did not wish to be left out of the effort by other 'fascists' to support the Spanish Nationalists, and a Legionary Unit was formed, which went to fight in Spain. In January 1937 Ion Mota and another prominent legionary, Vasile Marin, were killed there. Their funeral, in Bucharest a month later, was attended by official representatives of Germany, Italy, Spain, Portugal and Japan.

In the 1937 elections the Iron Guard, now called the 'All for the Fatherland' movement, by means of an electoral coalition with other right-wing parties, gained 16% of the votes, and more than 60 deputies. King Carol nevertheless called on others (the National Christian Party) to form a government. When, in February 1938, however, it became clear that the National Christian Party might be coming to some kind of arrangement with the Iron Guard, King Carol evicted the Premier, abolished the constitution, and suppressed party political activity, setting up a government under the Orthodox Patriarch. Codreanu was arrested, and sentenced to ten years' hard labour. He was murdered in prison (officially 'shot while attempting to escape').

Despite Codreanu's death, the Iron Guard remained a powerful force; and, amid the chaos of the 1939 situation (where Romania, which had relied in its foreign policy on playing off the Soviet Union and Germany, was faced with the results of the Nazi-Soviet Pact) it came to the fore once more. King Carol, under threat from many sides, seems to have seen the movement as a possible popular base. In June the Iron Guard formed the nucleus of a new national party to rule under a new constitution. Later that year Romania was dismembered, with extensive territory being ceded to Soviet Russia, Hungary and Bulgaria. King Carol abdicated and went abroad, and was succeeded by his son Michael, aged 19 (the actual ruler being General Antonescu). The Iron Guard unleashed a reign of terror, assassinating many prominent people. In January 1940 the Germans supported General Antonescu when he bloodily put down the Iron Guard, which had risen against the government, accusing it of selling out to the Germans. The Iron Guard ceased existence. At this point Romania finally became a puppet state of the Third Reich.

Where does all this place the Iron Guard? In the late Thirties, to enemies and allies alike, the movement appeared to be a typical example of 'international fascism'. The Guard's opposition to Germany in 1940 does not invalidate this, as the 'national' nature of fascism has always been taken to mean opposing, if necessary, foreign predators, however much they might be 'brothers in fascism'. But, despite the rhetoric of the Iron Guard in the late Thirties, which stressed its fraternity with the fascist governments of Germany, Italy and Spain, the main lines of its policy, as perceived in the writings of its leaders Codreanu and Mota, remained what it had always been – that of a reactionary Christian movement, devoted to anti-Semitism on the Eastern European model. Mota, describing the reasons for his mission to Spain, stressed not 'fascist' solidarity but 'Christian' solidarity (in line with Franco's rhetoric of the War as a Christian 'crusade'), and spoke of sacrificial death. Codreanu, in his writings, continued to concentrate on the Jewish threat. The Iron Guard had not changed from its profile of the nineteen-twenties; it was the concept of 'international fascism' that had changed.

1. Sir Oswald Mosley, 'The World Alternative', *Fascist Quarterly* 2/3 (1936), quoted in Griffin, op. cit., p. 175.
2. Henri Massis, *Chefs*, Paris, Plon, 1939, p. 150.
3. The Belgian Rexist José Streel, *La Révolution du vingtième siècle*, Brussels 1942, quoted in Griffin, op.cit., p. 206.
4. Georges Sorel, *Réflexions sur la violence*.
5. Robert Brasillach, *Notre Avant-guerre*, p. 362.
6. Ibid., p. 314.
7. Drieu la Rochelle, *Socialisme fasciste*, 1934, p. 179.
8. Walter Starkie, *The Waveless Plain*, London, 1938, pp. 408-9.
9. Sir Charles Petrie, *Lords of the Inland Sea*, London, 1937, p. 46.
10. See p. 35-7
11. Robert Brasillach, *Les Sept Couleurs*, 1939, p. 214.

12. Walter Starkie, 'Whither is Ireland heading – Is it Fascism? Thoughts on the Irish Free State', in *A Survey of Fascism* (CINEF Yearbook, 1928).

13. Eoin O'Duffy, speech to the League of Youth Organisation, O'Duffy section of Blueshirts, Mansion House, 16 November 1934. Quoted in Griffin, op.cit., pp. 182-4.

14. Eugen Weber, 'Romania', in *The European Right*, ed. Hans Rogger and Eugen Weber, Weidenfeld and Nicolson 1965, p. 517.

More Aspects of 'Fascism' in the Late Thirties

'A new kind of Socialism': newcomers from the Left

In the history of fascism, most of the major figures appear to have come originally from the Left. The Left-wing credentials of its most prominent theoretical forebear, Georges Sorel, underline its ambiguous Left-Right nature. Mussolini started as a Socialist; early German National Socialism was perceived as a Left-wing movement; even in England, the British Union of Fascists contained among its most prominent early members people who had started on the Left, especially former members of the Independent Labour Party (the left wing of the Labour movement).

In the mid-Thirties, however, a new influx to 'fascism' from the Left occurred, most prominently in France, in the form of philosophies and movements which, even if they did not describe themselves as 'fascist', are generally considered to have been so (to the extent that political scientists have often categorised them as more 'fascist' than many movements which called themselves by that title).

The largest and most successful of these movements was of course the *Parti Populaire Français* of Jacques Doriot, founded in 1936. Independently of this, however, a number of French Socialists, under the influence of the doctrines of the Belgian political philosopher Hendrik de Man, had in 1933 broken off from the SFIO (the French Socialist Party) to form a new group popularly called the 'néo-socialistes', which throughout the Thirties was to move gradually further to the Right.

De Man (1885-1953), originally a Belgian extreme Left-wing Socialist, had by the Twenties begun to question the tenets of

Marxism, which he attacked in his 1926 book *Towards a Psychology of Socialism*. As Sternhell describes it, 'the thought of Henri de Man pursued and developed that of Georges Sorel'.[1] Calling his new philosophy a 'revision of Marxism', de Man proposed a 'directed economy' governed by a strong state. By 1933, in his *Plan du Travail* ('Plan for work'), de Man was showing himself to be a precursor of what the French were to call 'le planisme', which was in essence a bringing up to date of the corporative policies of the old radical Right. For de Man, the middle classes were the key to achievement of true revolution, and shared with the working class a common enemy, Capitalism.

As early as 1930, Mussolini had perceived the affinity of de Man's ideas with the principles of Fascism. He wrote to de Man praising his writings. De Man, as Sternhell points out, showed in his reply, in a tone of 'historic complicity', that, while he did not hide his objections to some aspects of Fascism, he nevertheless was ready to accept what he saw as the positive sides of that doctrine:

> It is precisely because, belonging like you to the 'war gener-
> ation', and influenced like you by the ideas of Georges Sorel,
> I do not close my mind to any manifestation of creative
> force, it is precisely because I am not afraid to do justice to
> certain organisational aspects of Fascism, that I follow its
> progress with a passionate interest.[2]

De Man continued to see himself as a Socialist, however. His 1933 *Plan du Travail*, like Mosley's Memorandum, called for Keynesian deficit financing and for public works, to counteract the effects of the economic crisis. This policy, and that of the need for a central direction of the economy by a corporatist National Economic Council, were adopted by de Man's party, the Belgian Workers' Party, in the same year.

As a prominent member of this party, de Man held important ministerial posts between 1935 and 1937, and again from September 1939 to January 1940. Though these posts at one stage included that of Minister of Finance (1936-7), any effort to put his Plan into effect was frustrated, and, as with Mosley, that frustration seems to have led him to an impatience with parliamentary democracy, to the extent that when the Nazis marched in, he welcomed the opportunity this gave for a New Order in Europe, which would be based on a form of 'authoritarian socialism'. As early as June 1940, in a 'Manifesto to the Members of the Belgian Workers' Party', he acclaimed the victory of National Socialism as that of a new kind of Socialism on the European scale:

> The Socialist order will be realised [...] as the binding force of a national solidarity which will soon be continental if not world wide.[3]

De Man is important, above all, for the impetus he gave to other 'revisionist Socialists', particularly in France. Pre-eminent among these was Marcel Déat (1894-1955). A prominent member of the SFIO (the French Socialist Party), Déat had begun by the early Thirties to embrace ideas similar to those of de Man on the nature of the anti-capitalist battle, which was no longer to be built solely on the proletariat, but on a properly mobilised middle class. The solution to the economic crisis was to be 'étatist', based on co-operation between the classes. A strong state was the only way in which to counteract the forces of capital. His book *Perspectives socialistes* (1931) is generally accepted to have been the starting-point for what soon became known as 'neo-socialism'. In November 1933 Déat and various colleagues broke away from the Socialist Party, and founded a new party called the 'Parti Socialiste de France – Union Jean Jaurès', with 28 Deputies and 7 Senators. Léon Blum, the Socialist leader, had already raised the question, at the stormy Party Congress in July, of whether this new grouping was tinged with 'national socialism'.[4]

The new movement did not match up to its early success, and in November 1935 Déat founded a new movement, the 'Union Socialiste Républicaine'. After failing to win a seat in the 1936 elections, Déat devoted himself to journalism, and to the diffusion of his ideas. As war approached, he became a partisan of peace at any price. He also expressed far more open admiration for Nazi Germany.

The rest of the story is well known. Under the German Occupation, Déat became one of the most extreme collaborationists, violently opposed to the Vichy government, which he did not believe to be whole-hearted enough in its collaboration. In 1941 he founded yet another party, the 'Rassemblement National Populaire', which pursued friendship with the Germans.

As Sternhell has pointed out, even under the Occupation Déat still saw himself as a revolutionary socialist. Indeed, like de Man, he saw the German New Order for Europe as the best vehicle for the anti-capitalist renewal which had eluded him and others like him under the democratic system. Traditional Socialism, he pronounced, had been 'bathed in the democratic atmosphere of the nineteenth century and never grasped clearly the idea of what the true State had to be, namely a strong State, capable of instigating the revolution.' This new function of the State had been understood, and constructed, by Nazi Germany:

> The great novelty of the German State, the Third Reich, is that it succeeded in being both authoritarian and popular, so that it no longer expressed class interests, and offered something much better than a compromise between the interests of rival classes, or a precarious and constantly challenged balance between antagonistic forces. That was precisely the dangerous stage which our democracy had reached, leading to a visible paralysis of public institutions, a lack of authority, the breakdown of the State. This time the mass of the people was integrated into a national community in which social rank found its place without the hope of imposing its pre-eminence or dictatorship. Neither bourgeois capitalism nor the proletariat took over, so that the regime which emerged was tainted neither by Anglo-Saxon hypocrisies nor by Bolshevik brutalities. And the mass of workers ceased to be so much dust and instead took on organic form: it was plucked from its isolation and desolation, and integrated in the collective.[5]

It has been suggested that, in the Thirties, such tendencies had been less clearly manifested in the 'neo-Socialist' group. Nevertheless, though it must be admitted that the group never described itself as 'fascist', nor was considered as such by other politicians in the mid-Thirties (to the extent that Déat was given the post of Minister of Aviation in the Sarraut government of January-May 1936, and was accepted as a 'Popular Front' candidate for the May 1936 elections), the group's actual policies and philosophy, so closely based on de Man, were clearly already on a 'fascist' model.

Until the wartime experience, however, the activities of Déat and the 'neo-Socialists' had remained entirely within the democratic model. It is with Doriot's 'Parti Populaire Français' that we find the new surge from the Left embodied, in the Thirties, in a mass extra-parliamentary movement, which, unlike the 'neo-socialists', was for some time remarkably successful.

Jacques Doriot (1898-1945), as we have seen, broke with the Communist Party from 1934 onwards, though he succeeded in maintaining his control of his fief in Saint-Denis. For the next couple of years he continued to use the rhetoric of Communism. It is nevertheless now known that Doriot was already, in the years 1934-36, negotiating with, as Milza puts it, 'representatives of the economic world who were in search of a popular leader capable of heading an anti-Communist movement directed against the Popular Front'.[6] Prominent among these was Pierre Pucheu (later Minister of the Interior under Vichy). Already, Doriot's hatred of the Party that had rejected him had taken over; and, with the victory of the Popular Front in the May 1936 elections, he seems to have been ripe for a public change of political direction. In June of that year he founded the Parti Populaire Français (the French People's Party). Though, at first, ex-Communists were very prominent in its leadership, and though there was also considerable working-class support at this stage, soon a number of the more powerful members of the new movement came from the Right. Pucheu himself, for example, had been a member of Colonel La Roque's successful ex-service movement the Croix de Feu. The rhetoric of the PPF echoed many traditional themes of the French Right, particularly that of 'collaboration between the classes' as opposed to class warfare, and the 'solidarity of the family, the commune, the region, the firm, the profession, with, at the summit, the expression and synthesis of all the others, national solidarity'.[7] Soon the membership was attracting great sections of the middle classes, particularly those who, dispossessed by the economic crisis, found great attraction in a movement which combined anti-capitalism, anti-communism and 'patriotism'.

The PPF, even at its greatest extent of membership, probably did not exceed 300,000 members (far less that the main nationalist movement of the period, the 'Croix de Feu', which by this time had become a respectable party working within the parliamentary system, calling itself the Parti Social Français). But its 'clout' was greater than its numbers suggest. French industry, and French economic circles (including the banks) initially gave it discreet support, and, more publicly, a whole wave of 'intellectuals' came out in support of the movement. Alongside the movement's most successful publicist, the prominent novelist and journalist mentioned above, Pierre Drieu la Rochelle (1893-1945) (who enthusiastically hailed the 'leader' who was going to transform the French political scene), other intellectual converts included Alfred Fabre-Luce, Bertrand de Jouvenel, Ramon Fernandez, Abel Bonnard and the political scientist Maurice Duverger.

Like many fascist movements (and many populist movements of the Right then and since), Doriot's movement, despite its support from big business, claimed to be the great defender of the small businessman against the great combines, the lower middle classes against the upper middle classes. It also claimed to stand for a new society, while acting as a prop for the old. Doriot and his followers claimed not to be 'fascists'. But the rhetoric was fascist, and so were the outward signs and symbols of the movement as they developed. There were mass meetings, at which members performed a form of the 'fascist salute', and at which the 'party flag' – a Celtic cross – took on a highly symbolic role; there was an oath of loyalty to 'the Leader', whose powerful oratory was renowned; and there was a party uniform. Anti-Semitism soon, in the French tradition, took on a prominent role.

In October 1938 a number of the Party's leading supporters left it. They included Pucheu, Paul Marion, Drieu la Rochelle, Fabre-Luce and many others. Motivation appears to have been mixed, with some objecting to Doriot's attitude to the Munich settlement, and others experiencing a general disillusionment with Doriot as leader, both because of his political ineffectiveness and because of the disorder of his personal life. In August 1939, when Doriot was mobilised into the army, the party went into further decline. It might have seemed that the last had been seen of Doriot's political career. Under the Occupation, however, Doriot became an arch-collaborator, and also revived the PPF. He was the driving force behind the 'Légion des Volontaires Français contre le Bolchévisme' (the Legion of French Volunteers against Bolshevism, or the LVF), to form a fighting unit alongside the Germans on the Russian Front. Like Degrelle, he himself fought there in German uniform. At the end of the war, having fled from France to Germany, he was killed by a British aircraft which strafed the staff car in which he was travelling.

The advent of these new 'fascist' movements from the Left, in the Thirties, was mainly a Belgian and French phenomenon; but there was an odd, unsuccessful, British attempt at copying them. This was the British People's Party, founded in April 1939. The main protagonists were Ben Greene, a former Labour candidate who was prominent in Right-wing and pro-Nazi circles, and John Beckett, a former member of the ILP who had been a member of Mosley's British Union of Fascists. Beckett appears to have wished the new movement, alongside an anti-war policy, to be based strongly on social reform. Much of the rhetoric was similar to that of Doriot's PPF, whose name was so clearly reflected in the new movement's. The avowed aims included 'the right to security and social justice', the abolition of 'all forms of land spec-ulation', the security of labour in its industrial organisation', and 'the abolition of all class differences'.

This new party had, however, a further agenda, based on racism. Among the other declared aims of the movement were 'the abolition of a financial system based upon usury which perpetuates social and economic injustice', and 'safeguarding the employment and integrity of the British people against alien influence and infiltration'. In the Hythe by-election of July 1939 (which the BPP fought, its candidate being H. St John Philby, the father of Kim Philby), the BPP showed its true colours by the anti-Semitic nature of some of its propaganda. Its main theme was, however, avoidance by hook or by crook of war with Germany.

The BPP was a small and insignificant example of a trend which had one of its most powerful incarnations in Doriot's PPF. The new Thirties influx from the Left, while usually not calling itself 'fascist', nevertheless, in some of its most prominent incar-

nations, exhibited more traits of what was popularly considered
to be 'fascism' than many of the movements that flaunted that
name.

Anti-Semitism and fascism

Anti-Semitism has, for the past two centuries, been a dominant
and wide-ranging force. While some of its most virulent manifestations have been found in central and Eastern Europe, it has
also played a significant part in a country like France – and even
in England.[8]

Politically, anti-Semitism played a major role in what we have
called French 'pre-fascism' of the period 1880-1914, and it
remained a prominent feature of the French extra-parliamentary
Right, and in particular of Action Française, right through the
inter-war period. In large part this anti-Semitism was based on
the 'Jew as capitalist' and 'Jew as dominator of society' models,
though containing elements of 'protection of the national
culture'; by the Thirties, the myth of the 'Judaeo-Bolshevik plot'
had become part of the stock-in-trade of the extreme Right in the
Western democracies. The German 'radical Right' movements,
including the Nazis, were imbued with anti-Semitism which was
more concerned with the purity of the race, but also containing
elements of these other strands.

Given the prevalence of anti-Semitism among movements of
the 'radical Right', it is somewhat ironic that the movement
which gave its name to 'fascism', Italian Fascism, should, as we
have seen, have been originally so free of this tendency. Anti-
Semitism had not, in fact, been very prevalent in Italy up to this
time, despite the Jews' prominence in business, banking and the
professions; and the members of the comparatively small Jewish
community in Italy had become to a large extent assimilated into
the national life. Charles Delzell and Roger Eatwell, among
others, have shown the part that Jews played in the early years
of Italian Fascism. In the early Thirties Mussolini was at times
heard to express disgust at Hitler's racism.

The other great exception, among regimes of the radical Right,
was Salazar's Estado Novo, in Portugal. As Tom Gallagher has
put it, though 'ultra-Rightists moulded by Action Française or
keen to emulate the latest trends from Nazi Germany ventilated

anti-Semitic sentiments', the government did not encourage such 'random outbursts':

> Salazar did not go in for systematic persecution of social minorities. As persecution of the German Jews was set up during the late nineteen-thirties, he publicly dissociated himself from anti-Semitism. In 1938 the press was allowed to criticise Nazi persecution of the Jews and, in a small but telling gesture, the government bought a disused synagogue in Tomar [...] and turned it into a Jewish museum. Samuel Schwarz, the Polish Jew who had restored the building, was given Portuguese citizenship in 1939, one year before many Jews fleeing the Nazi terror were warmly welcomed in Lisbon.[9]

Nevertheless, when it travelled abroad even in the early days, the Italian 'fascist idea' did prove attractive to prominent anti-Semites in other countries. In the Twenties the CINEF (Centre International des Études Fascistes), for example, alongside its naïve enthusiasts, counted among the members of its Council the inveterate anti-Semites H. de Vries de Heekelingen (from Holland) and Lord Sydenham of Combe (from England). And other movements of a virulently anti-Semitic nature, such as the Imperial Fascist League, took their name and their apparent inspiration from an Italy that was comparatively blameless in this respect.

The advent of the Nazis to prominence in the period from 1929 onwards, and to power in 1933, provided a powerful impetus for the anti-Semitic element in 'fascism'. Among the reasons for this may well have been the realisation of what a powerful force anti-Semitism could be for arousing the people. In Britain, for example, Sir Oswald Mosley's British Union of Fascists, which at the start had shown little sign of this tendency, emerged in late 1934, in response to a loss of respectable public support, as a major anti-Semitic force. Within a short time, the movement was to change its name to the 'British Union of Fascists and National Socialists'.

In Eastern Europe, of course, movements such as the Romanian Iron Guard had been strongly anti-Semitic from the start; and the Scandinavian and Baltic countries, in particular, appear to have been strongly attracted by the Nazi form of 'racial anti-Semitism' based on the superiority of the Nordic races.

As the War approached, and German influence became stronger on the international scene, even the exceptions (apart from Salazar's Portugal) began to fall in line with Nazi racist policies. We have seen how Horthy's Hungary, for example, began in 1938, as it became increasingly dependent on Nazi Germany, to produce harsh anti-Semitic laws that went way beyond that regime's previous, admittedly anti-Semitic, agenda.

The big turn-around, however, was that which took place in Mussolini's Italy. Here, in 1938, a number of Nazi-style anti-Semitic decrees were produced, and anti-Semitism became a doctrinal part of Fascism. What caused this? Though commentators have suggested that Mussolini was in part 'programmed' for such a change by the 'racist' theories of some of his propagandists during the Abyssinian War, there is little doubt that the crucial factor was that (after many differences with Hitler in relation to the European political scene) Mussolini had been coming increasingly under the influence of the German dictator, and wished to show solidarity with his new ally.

Typically, however, the new decrees, though they brought significant hardship to a number of people, tended to be carried out negligently – or, one might put it, in a spirit of moderation. Italy certainly remained one of the areas where the Jews were better treated during the war years – to the extent that in 1942-3 the Italian Zone of France served as a refuge for Jews escaping from the French authorities' policy of deporting them as part of the 'Final Solution'. It was when, after the fall of Mussolini, the Germans marched into the Italian-occupied zone of France and into Northern Italy, that the Italian Jews faced their greatest trials. Even so, over 80% of Italian Jews survived, often aided by the Italian population.

In our definition of fascism (if we were to attempt such a thing) anti-Semitism would appear, on the basis of its widespread presence from the late nineteenth century onwards in most of the movements of the 'radical Right' and of inter-war 'fascism', to be one of the major characteristics. As with all such generalisations, however, there are important exceptions – and in this case the most important exception is the founder of the concept 'fascism', the Italian regime up to 1938.

*

By the late Thirties, a wide array of movements became associated with the term 'international fascism'. Some had pre-existed the appearance of the concept, but, given its success, eagerly associated themselves with it. Others were formed under the influence of the examples of Italian Fascism and German Nazism, while 'Catholic fascism', in particular, derived in large part from the long-lasting model of Action Française. As the Thirties wore on, however, most of these movements became more and more influenced by the success of Nazism, and began to take on an increasing number of its characteristics, including the Nazis' racist policies in relation to the Jews and other minorities. The experience of war was to highlight these trends even more.

1. Sternhell, *Ni droite ni gauche*, p. 156.

2. Letter from Henri de Man to Mussolini, 23 August 1930, quoted in Sternhell, *Ni droite ni gauche*, pp. 50-1.

3. Quoted in Philip Rees, *Biographical Dictionary of the Extreme Right since 1890*, pp. 86-7.

4. Speech of Blum, 20 July 1933, quoted in Sternhell, op.cit., p. 213.

5. Marcel Déat, 'L'État et la Révolution', *L'Oeuvre*, November 1943, quoted in Griffin, *Fascism*, p. 201.

6. Pierre Milza, *Les Fascismes*, Seuil 1991, p. 351.

7. Jacques Doriot, *Refaire la France* (The Remaking of France), quoted in Ste4rnhell, *Ni droite ni gauche*, p. 203.

8. See, e.g., Colin Holmes, *Anti-Semitism in British Society*, Arnold 1979, and Richard Griffiths, *Patriotism Perverted: Captain Ramsay, the Right Club, and British Anti-Semitism 1939-40*, Constable 1998.

9. Tom Gallagher, 'Conservatism, Dictatorship and Fascism in Portugal, 1914-45', in Martin Blinkhorn (ed.), *Fascists and Conservatives*, Unwin Hyman 1990, p. 166.

9

'A Great Political Alliance'

Fascism and the War

It was Vidkun Quisling, whose name has come to stand for treason and betrayal, who used the phrase 'a great political alliance' to describe his vision for Norway's future in the new Europe. Nationalistic as the individual 'fascist' movements in the different countries of Europe had appeared, the quasi-unanimity with which they adhered to the concept of a New Order for Europe (under German domination), when faced by the apparent invincibility of German arms, is striking. In all the occupied countries, indigenous fascists emerged to collaborate with the conqueror. In Belgium, Léon Degrelle and José Streel of the Rexist movement welcomed the 'crystallisation of what historians will call the century of fascism or national socialism'[1], and de Man acclaimed a 'Socialist order' which would 'soon be continental if not world wide'.[2] In France, Drieu la Rochelle declared that the revolution that was taking place in Europe was a 'revolution of the soul'; Déat proclaimed that a new France was about to be created, integrated into Europe, with collaboration being 'neither a material necessity, nor a provisional expedient, but a fundamental doctrine'[3]; and Doriot, like Degrelle, was prepared to defend fascist Europe by donning the uniform of the SS. In Norway, Quisling, feeling that the Norwegian people needed 'to rise again as a national and free people within the new Europe, and that 'the new Norway must build on Germanic principles'[4], had even gone so far as to visit Copenhagen in April 1940 to assist the German invasion of Norway by passing on vital information. In Holland, Anton Mussert of the *Nationaal-socialistische Beweging* wrote a letter to Hitler on 27 August 1940, calling for a New Order of Nordic nations, in the form of a federation. And there were many others.

There were, of course, exceptions to this pattern. An individual's pre-war 'fascist' activities did not necessarily pre-ordain him to be a collaborator. Thus, in France, Georges Valois of *Le Faisceau*, who joined the Resistance, eventually died in Bergen-Belsen concentration camp.

Attitudes that had been taken to Germany before the war were no pointer to subsequent action. Those people who, while extremely 'fascist' in their outlook, had been lukewarm or even hostile to the German experiment, now found occasion swiftly to revise their attitudes.

The French fascist Robert Brasillach is an illustration of this. In his volume of reminiscences of the pre-war period, *Notre Avant-guerre*, published in Paris in 1941, he used a lot of material from his pre-war writings; and a study of the apparently minor changes he now made to these texts is revealing. At one point in his 1939 novel *Les Sept couleurs*, for example, Brasillach had run through the various European forms of fascism, finishing up by declaring the Spanish Civil War to be the highest point in their development. Admitting that one must 'admire the practical achievements' of Nazism, he nevertheless asserted that it lacked a 'religious, Catholic, fraternal' dimension; and he went on to suggest that 'Spain may astonish the world, if she so wishes [...] by installing a kind of fascist Catholicism'. In the 1941 version, which closely followed the 1939 text, this short section was completely cut out, and the emphasis was laid on the German experiment, as Brasillach had seen it at the 1937 Nuremberg Rally. Here again, however, the emphasis had been completely changed. In 1937 he had found the new Germany 'strange', and 'a great historical curiosity'; the impression was one of uncertainty and even of a need to defend oneself against what was going on. All this was removed from the 1941 text, often very subtly. To take one example: pre-war, he had written of the Nuremberg ceremonies, 'It is because these ceremonies and these songs mean something that we must pay attention to them, and think how to ward off what they signify'; in 1941, this became simply 'It is because these ceremonies and these songs mean something that we must pay attention to them'. There are many other such changes.[5] By 1941 Brasillach saw Hitler and the Nazis as the future for Europe. His changes to his texts, which now

acclaimed the Nazi regime as the most important manifestation of 'fascism', were unlikely to have been caused merely by
concern for the censor.

It would, however, be wrong to see all movements of the Right,
in the occupied countries, as being in favour of whole-hearted
collaboration, to the extent of willing a German victory. Vichy
France is a case in point. Though Marshal Pétain's regime was
cast in the mould of the Action Française radical Right; though
its core anti-Semitism was such that its Jewish legislation in
1940 preceded any German demands, and was more stringent
than the legislation produced by the Germans in the Occupied
Zone of France; though Vichy also attracted many ex-Doriot or
'planiste' Right-wingers such as Pucheu, who was Interior
Minister in 1941; and though the corporatist element in the
regime came fully to the forefront with the *Charte du Travail* of
October 1941; Vichy's attitude towards the occupier was on the
whole one of trying to negotiate and to 'come to accommodations', but not one of embracing the New Order for Europe, as
the 'Paris collaborators' such as Doriot and Déat had done. Vichy
remained devoted to what it believed to be the interests of
France, even if its leaders too facilely interpreted those interests
as being furthered by collaboration with the foreign power which
had defeated them, and even if their innate anti-Semitism and
lack of concern for humanity made them participate, from 1942
onwards, in the deportation of Jews as part of the 'Final
Solution'.

Vichy is a very good example, but almost the only one, of a
'radical Right' body failing fully to embrace the New Order. It is
important to stress, though, that those (including the present
author in his 1970 *Marshal Pétain*) who have seen a fundamental
contrast between the 'conservatism' of Vichy and the 'radicalism'
of the Nazis and the Paris collaborators, have been to a large
extent wrong (misled not only by the 'Rémond' definition of
Action Française, but also by the wartime comments of Otto
Abetz, the German ambassador to Vichy France). In the preface
to the 1994 edition of *Marshal Pétain*, I rectified this by stating
that there were indeed serious differences of politics and policy
between Paris collaboration and Vichy, but that it had been
wrong to categorise too rigidly, when it came to assessing the
nature of their Right-wing views:

There were of course differences between the two, which were stressed by such ideologues of National Socialism as Abetz [...] Similarly, John Amery, the future Free Corps member, a Doriot fan who visited Vichy in its first year, voiced the Parisian collaborators' disgust with what appeared to be a backward-looking, conservative regime. Such interested parties depicted the edges in too hard a way, however. Vichy and 'fascism' also had much in common.[6]

One thing is clear for Europe as a whole, however. While there were a number of 'fascists', in each country, who opposed the invader, or who, while attempting an accommodation with him nevertheless kept a distance, the predominant trend was towards outright collaboration, and an acceptance of the European 'New Order'. And by 1942, when the Final Solution policies for the extermination of the Jews were coming fully into effect, such people either tacitly accepted what was happening (while certainly not abandoning their allegiance to the New Order), or, as in the case of the Vichy government, actively participated in the rounding-up of Jews for deportation. Later professions of ignorance as to what was going to happen to the Jews hold no water. Even if the detail of the extermination camps was not known, it was clear that the Jews were being sent to some terrible fate, with parents being separated from their children, and with conditions in the trains carrying 'Judenstoff' (Jewish material – the terrible dehumanising Nazi term used in their documents) being appalling.

This, more than anything else, has influenced the post-war concept of what 'fascism' was. Where we, studying the Thirties, have become aware of the great diversity that sheltered under that umbrella, the wartime experience has meant that most people in our own time envisage 'fascism' as having been a monolith dominated by, and in the image of, German National Socialism.

Indeed, in this post-war vision of fascism and the Thirties there has been a tendency to classify Italian Fascism, from the start, as having been an adjunct of Nazism (whereas it was only the war that made it so). The differences between Mussolini and Hitler in the mid-Thirties are forgotten, as are the presumptions of the politicians in England and France that Mussolini might be able to serve as a bulwark against Nazism. Having for a time attempted a balancing-act between Germany and the Western democracies, Mussolini had attached his star to that of Germany by the immediate pre-war years, and was, after his declaration of war at the time of the Fall of France in 1940, militarily bound to Germany, without whose aid the invasion of Greece would have been a disaster, and the North African campaign would have been even worse. The war made Italy the weaker partner in what had been supposed to be an alliance of equals, which was now dominated by the military efficiency of Germany.

It was in Italy, however, that the war provided the final twist in the history of fascism, when, in the Salò Republic (1943-45), Mussolini appeared to return to many of the guiding principles of his first incarnation as a fascist (before his advent to power), to the extent that some observers have suggested that the Salò Republic was 'the nearest approach to a fascist state (in the true sense of the term) to have existed'.

The Salò Republic

After the Allied invasion of Sicily and then mainland Italy in July 1943, many leading Fascists wished to withdraw from the war. The Fascist Grand Council, on 25 July, passed by 19 votes to 7 a motion that some of Mussolini's powers should be taken from him, and that the King should become Commander-in-chief and the main decision-taker. Later on the 25th, the King summoned Mussolini and informed him that he was replacing him with Marshal Badoglio as head of government. Mussolini was then arrested.

Badoglio set about negotiating for peace with the Allies, and on 8 September he accepted General Eisenhower's unconditional surrender terms. The Germans rushed troops into Italy. On 13 September Mussolini was rescued by the Germans, from a hotel in the Apennines where he was being held, in a raid by Otto Skorzeny's glider-borne commando force. He was taken to Germany, but was almost immediately returned to Northern Italy, now occupied by the Germans, to set up a new State called the Italian Social Republic, based in Salò.

The Salò Republic was an attempt to break with the recent past. Some of its supporters even suggested doing away with the name 'Fascist', because of the disrepute into which its Grand Council had brought it; but Mussolini insisted on its retention. The Party of the new State was therefore called the 'Fascist Republican Party'. Among the leading figures in the new Party were Guido Buffarini-Guidi (Minister of the Interior), who had been a strong critic of the increasing bureaucracy of the Fascist State in the early nineteen-forties; Nicola Bombacci, a former communist who had joined the Fascists in the nineteen-twenties, hoping for an alliance between the two creeds; and Alessandro Pavolini, an extreme radical who was also strongly pro-Nazi. Those who had voted against Mussolini at the Grand Council, and who were captured in the new Republic, were executed (including Mussolini's son-in-law Ciano).

At the first Congress of the new Party, at Verona in November 1943, the Manifesto put forward a number of radical proposals. Much of this reflected the original principles of Fascism, but, as Griffin has pointed out, it was in fact a strange mixture of the old and the new. To revolutionary socialism and Republican ultra-nationalism were added anti-Semitism and Catholicism.[7] On the negative side, the 'treachery of the last King' was evoked to justify the creation of a Republic; and it was promised that the large fortunes made under the twenty years of Fascist rule would be investigated. Also, the 'elimination of the centuries-old British intrigues from our continent' was promised, and 'those belonging to the Jewish faith' would 'for the duration of this war' be regarded as belonging 'to an enemy nationality'. The immediate goal was 'the unity, independence and territorial integrity of the Fatherland within its maritime and Alpine frontiers'.[8]

The radical internal policies included: a programme of nationalisation; the division of uncultivated or non-producing land among labourers; the creation of worker-owned farming co-operatives; the setting-up of corporatist management councils of employers and workers; 'planning'; and 'profit-sharing'.[9]

Whatever the social policies of the Salò Republic (whose Fascist Republican Party is believed to have attracted about half a million members), its main characteristics were to be governed by the war situation. Fighting with the partisans became particularly bitter, and the regime's efforts were directed towards their ever more bloody and violent suppression. The Germans, who ruled *de facto* in the area, were little interested in social reform, but above all concerned with measures to help the war effort: rounding-up of Italians for forced labour in Germany, ensuring of factory production for the war effort, keeping down of dissidents in the population, ensuring of defence, and so on. The fate of the Jews in the area, vast numbers of whom were deported, was not solely due to German pressure, however; the regime had already branded them as enemies of the State.

The Salò Republic lasted for a year and a half. It was ended by the Allied advance. In April 1945 the fleeing Mussolini was captured by partisans, and shot.

The avowed aims of the Salò Republic were more radical than anything produced by 'fascists' when in power, and had far more in common with the ideals of those 'fascist' movements which never achieved power. The fact that these aims, in the wartime situation, were never brought to fruition, leaves one to wonder what would have happened if the Republic had survived. Certainly there can have been no material advantage to Mussolini in the return to the original ideals of Fascism at that point in the war. It was as though he had realised with regret all the compromises of the last twenty years. At all events, the Salò Republic is an extraordinary addition to our gallery of variants of fascism.

1. José Streel, *La Révolution du vingtième siècle* (*The Revolution of the Twentieth Century*), Brussels 1942, quoted in Griffin, op. cit., p. 207.

2. Quoted in Philip Rees, op. cit., p. 86-7.

3. *L'Oeuvre*, 5 July 1940, quoted in Pascal Ory, *Les Collaborateurs 1940-1945*, Seuil 1976, p. 107.

4. *Quisling calls Norway*, Munich 1942, quoted in Griffin, op.cit., p. 211.

5. For a detailed examination of these texts, see Richard Griffiths, 'Brasillach et la révolution fasciste' in Harris and Wetherill (eds.), *Littérature et révolutions en France*, Rodopi, Amsterdam, 1991, pp. 195-226.

6. Richard Griffiths, *Marshal Pétain*, Constable 1994, p. xviii.

7. Roger Griffin, *Fascism*, p. 86.

8. Verona Manifesto of the Fascist republican Party, quoted in Griffin, op.cit., pp. 86-7.

9. See Griffin, op.cit., and Roger Eatwell, *Fascism: a History*, p. 84.

10

Race, Nostalgia and the Search for Acceptance

The Post-War Extreme Right

In the immediate post-war period, most pre-war fascists and fascist movements were forced into hiding or anonymity, for two very good reasons: (i) in most of the occupied countries, pre-war fascists had been among the most fervent collaborators, and were now seen as traitors; (ii) the discovery of the appalling details of the Final Solution policies, the Holocaust of the Jewish people, as carried out from early 1942 onwards, tarred all 'fascists' with the same brush, that of Nazi racist exterminators.

Prominent fascists were severely dealt with. Among those who were executed for treason were Vidkun Quisling (Norway), Anton Mussert (Holland), José Streel (Belgium), Guido Buffarini-Guidi (Italy)*, Robert Brasillach (France), and William Joyce (Great Britain). Charles Maurras, aged 83, was condemned to solitary confinement for life. Drieu la Rochelle committed suicide before he could be captured. Others were condemned to death *in absentia*, but managed to escape to other countries where they were often aided to remain undetected: Léon Degrelle (Belgium) and Xavier Vallat (France), for example, took refuge in Spain; Marcel Déat (France) hid in a convent in Turin until his death (as a Catholic convert) in 1955; Hendrik de Man (Belgium) took refuge in Switzerland; Alphonse de Chateaubriant (France) lived in Austria under a false name till his death in 1951; and so on. The movements to which they had belonged disappeared.

---

* Mussolini's Salò Republic having been treasonous towards the Italian war effort, once Italy had re-entered the war on the side of the Allies.

Many of the ordinary members of them had a very difficult time in the immediate post-war years, as did members of other, non-fascist movements (such as the Breton and Flemish nationalists) who had perceived an advantage to their cause in collaboration with the Germans. Indeed, in countries like France the whole Right came under suspicion, to the extent that even moderate Right-wingers found themselves initially forced to join parties of Centrist or Left complexion.

At the same time, fascism became inadmissible not just for national reasons, but because of the wave of revulsion that spread across Europe at the Nazi atrocities, and at the complicity in them on the part of fascists in all the occupied countries. Many pre-war fascists may have kept their opinions: but mostly they hid them, and often joined more conventional parties, while those who tried to start new parties on the old lines (from which the word 'fascist' was conspicuously absent) found very little popular support. 'The war', in Roberto Chiarini's words, 'bankrupted Nazism and Fascism as viable ideologies'.[1]

In these circumstances the word 'fascist' began to take on its more general post-war function as a term of generalised abuse, the 'hold-all' epithet described in our Introduction. 'Fascism' itself appeared to have disappeared as a political force.

Only in Spain and Portugal did the pre-war regimes continue. They were regularly described as 'fascist' by those in other countries, even though the term now had so much less of a precise meaning. In fact, both regimes tempered their pre-war attitudes considerably. In Spain, as Paul Preston has pointed out,

> After 1945, the pragmatic rightists who, despite their discomfort at the Falange's anti-oligarchical fascist rhetoric, had been content to be part of the Movimiento in its most pro-Axis phase, proclaimed themselves monarchist, Carlist, Christian democrat or just plain Catholic. To their relief, the regime made serious efforts after 1945 to sever its links with a fascist past.[2]

In Portugal, 1945 found the *Estado Novo* being proclaimed to be an 'organic democracy', and opposition candidates were allowed to stand, for the first time, in the elections. Though, behind these outward signs, Salazar was cracking down even more firmly on internal opposition, these changes do show a desire to distance himself from his 'international fascist' past.

The Portuguese regime lasted till 1974, when it was toppled by a revolution. In 1975 Franco died, having prepared the way for a seamless transition to a constitutional monarchy.

In Germany and Austria, of course, many former Nazis were tried as war criminals, but many of the rank and file (such had been the wide membership of the Party) escaped punishment. The victorious Allies had expected their occupying forces in Germany to face post-war Nazi resistance, but this did not develop. Instead, former party members became an integral part of the institutions of the new democracy in West Germany.

So, in the immediate post-war years, it must have seemed that the extreme Right in a 'fascist' mould had no place in the new Europe. In the last quarter of the century, however, new forms of an extreme Right have not only appeared, but in certain areas have had considerable success. To describe them, the term 'Neo-Fascism' has been coined. To what extent is this a valid term?

Neo-Fascism?

Though, in the immediate post-war period, a number of small parties of the extreme Right grew up in most countries of Europe, they were remarkably unsuccessful, and attracted only an infinitesimally small portion of the population in each case. It was in the Sixties that successful movements of the extreme Right began to emerge across Europe; and since that time there have been frequent Press 'scares' about the possible advent to power of such movements – a fear that recently became reality with the success of Jörg Haider's Freedom Party in Austria.

If the playing-field were level, there would I suppose be no harm in calling such parties 'neo-fascist'. The 'neo' part could establish that this was not the same thing as 'fascism', but that there were a number of features in common. The more popular usage of the word 'fascism' as a general term of abuse in the post-war period has meant, however, that the term can only muddy the waters for the general public (and indeed for specialists) when it is applied to political movements.

That all these movements are manifestations of an extreme

Right is clear. But what kind of extreme Right? And to what extent are they all similar to each other?

There is even more of a difference between the various manifestations of the extremist Right in different countries in our time, than there was between the different movements of the 'radical Right' in the inter-war era. On the one hand one has populist and often fragmented neo-Nazi movements, across not just Europe but the world, which specialise in the accoutrements and external characteristics of Nazism and in 'Holocaust denial'. Then there are 'intellectual' movements such as the French 'Nouvelle Droite'. Then there are the more successful movements on a national scale, such as Le Pen's *Front National* in France, the *Movimento Sociale Italiano* (MSI) and its successor the *Alleanza Nazionale* (AL) in Italy, the *Republikaner* (REP) in Germany, and Jörg Haider's Freedom Party in Austria. Each of these, in turn, seems fundamentally different from the others.

There are only two things which seem to permeate almost all these different manifestations of the Right (in differing quantities), and those are nostalgia and racism. These are tempered, in the more successful parties on the national scale, by a pragmatic realisation that these parties need acceptance by a large proportion of the population – a population which is far less open to 'fascist' ideas than the peoples of pre-war Europe had been.

While it is understandable that a nostalgia for the trappings of the 'glorious' past should be central to some of the movements that have emerged in Germany, Austria and Italy, it is more surprising to find such a widespread nostalgia for Hitler and the Nazis outside these countries, on international websites of Nazi memorabilia and in the detailed paraphernalia surrounding so many of the new movements of the extreme Right. This obsession with Hitler and his movement make the modern 'neo-fascists' very different from their predecessors in the Thirties, whose central concerns were usually national and/or ideological, and looked forwards rather than backwards. Often, the symbolic connections seem almost trivial. In Britain, for example, Jordan and Tyndall's National Socialist Movement (later the British Movement) was founded on the anniversary of Hitler's birthday in 1962, and the 'Combat 18' movement, founded in the early Nineties, takes its title from the initials of Adolf Hitler's name, the first and eighth letters in the alphabet.

Such extremist movements, across Europe, all share a racism
that is fed by Holocaust denial; as Roger Eatwell has put it, they
seem to want to have their cake and eat it: 'What is said in public
("we have been misled about the Holocaust") may not reflect an
internal agenda ("come back Hitler and racism")'.[3] So, here, the
legacy of the Thirties seems to be a particularly narrow one,
based on the admiration felt by the immature and the alienated
for a movement that appears to have the allure of being the
extreme of evil. There is also, in these movements, a tacit acceptance that their destiny is to remain a minority interest.

In Germany and Austria, the nostalgia is more real; it is felt
for a movement that was supported by many, and by the fathers
of even more. Here the term 'neo-Nazi' does in fact have some
meaning. But the most extreme expressions of this nostalgia are
found in the violent and militant movements which, already
strong in the Eighties, have now been swelled by the ferocious
neo-Nazism manifesting itself in the former East Germany. The
excessive racism of these people is expressed in the terrorising of
the immigrant community.

Racism has always been a potent force in Europe, and the
extreme Right has found a fertile ground in the new targets for
such racism that have emerged – the Turkish guest-workers in
Germany, the formerly Algerian 'beurs' in France. Much popular
support can be gained by appealing to those who feel most threatened by such immigrants, particularly the populations of the
areas in which they settle, whose livelihoods and way of life often
seem threatened.

This nostalgia, and this racism, however, can have an
ambiguous role for those more successful movements that wish
to progress to a more prominent role in national politics. One
finds a certain amount of 'hedging' coming into play. In Italy, the
MSI's nostalgia had of course been for Mussolini. Giorgio
Almirante, who became its leader from 1969 onwards, had been
a prominent member of Mussolini's Salò Republic. Almost as
soon as he took over the party, however, he set about changing
the party image, aiming to 'make his party look modern, law-
abiding and respectable in order to widen its appeal and end its
isolation'. This he largely succeeded in doing; but, like most
parties of the extreme Right which have attempted this transfor-
mation, the MSI also had to try to keep its original support as

well. Thus, while an image of non-violence was being projected, fascist trappings being discouraged, and the rhetoric being purged, street violence in fact continued. The greatest need, however, was to persuade the old supporters that the aim was the same, even if the image had changed. Luciano Cheles has brilliantly shown how the visual material used in the MSI's posters and literature skilfully incorporated images (allusions to Mussolini and the Fascist past) which could be understood by the faithful, but which would be unnoticed by others.[4]

The party that grew out of the MSI, Fini's *Alleanza Nazionale*, which was to gain 105 Deputies and 43 Senators in the March 1994 elections, went even further in the direction of an appeal to the Centre. As Roberto Chiarini has put it:

Blackshirts and Roman salutes vanished. Fascism was consigned to the 'judgement of historians'. The old watchwords of the 'alternative to the system', of 'going beyond liberal capitalism and social-communism', in the name of a corporatist and social 'third way', and of the 'historic and political continuity with the Fascist movement' – watchwords which had in fact been strongly reiterated at the Rimini conference of 1990 – were forgotten. In their place came unreserved praise for the market (freed from all administrative restraints), for individual initiative (to be encouraged by tax relief on investment), for an ostentatious rediscovery of previously neglected values like 'freedom, democracy and solidarity', and for a rejection of 'any form of dictatorship or totalitarianism' and of 'any form of racism or discrimination'.[5]

As Chiarini goes on to say, 'Only time will tell if this policy overhaul is cosmetic and opportunistic or, instead, the first step towards a complete integration into the democratic fold'. The same could be said of most of the other attempts at treading this particular highwire; for example, in Germany, where the leader of the *Republikaner*, Franz Schönhuber, and many of his early followers, were former members of the Waffen-SS. Though Schönhuber's platform was based on nationalism and on fomenting discontent with the influx of foreigners and ethnic Germans from the East into Germany (with highly explosive anti-Turkish material being used in his 1989 campaign), he nevertheless, in interviews, expressly played down his Nazi past, stating:

> I have no Nazi past. I regard the National Socialist State as absolutely incompatible with the rule of law. Racism and fascism led us into the most horrible catastrophe in our national history.[6]

Ironically, the reunion of East and West Germany led to a decline in the fortunes of the REP (but at the same time a growth in extremist violence from splinter groups). Only where the REP was able to harness current dissatisfactions (unemployment, immigration, discontent with the performance of the major parties), has it been able to serve as the vehicle for 'protest votes' from people who would never consider themselves to have 'Nazi' tendencies, but who have presumably been lulled by the more emollient public statements, on this score, produced by the party.

Nowhere is the success of such ambiguous approaches more evident than in Austria, where Jörg Haider's party succeeded in cashing in on the widespread dissatisfaction with the consensus governments that had ruled the country for so many years, and against which there had until now seemed to be no redress. Haider, like Rightists in other countries, has played to two constituencies. On the one hand, he has made statements to reunions of war veterans (including former SS) which reassure them about the patriotic role they had played in the war. On the other hand, he has publicly disavowed what he had said at such gatherings, and has spoken of devotion to the democratic system, etc. Here, the combination of these two essentially incompatible ingredients has led his party to power in a Right-wing coalition. Only time will tell (to mimic Chiarini's words) whether the public statements will turn out to have been cosmetic, or to have been a solid commitment to democratic values.

If anything were to underline the basic differences between the various national Right-wing parties, however, the French *Front National* would do so. Its unprecedented run (until recently) of successes made of it probably the most successful of all French movements of the radical Right. Its major force has come from anti-immigrant policies; but it has also taken much of its strength from being the last of a line of domestic 'radical Right' movements, based in nationalism, 'la terre et les morts', Catholicism, and a tension between radicalism and traditionalism, that has stretched from Barrès, Maurras, and Action Française, through the fascist 'leagues' of the Thirties and the PPF, to the present (a lineage which the FN itself proudly proclaims).

It is typical of modern scholarship relating to the Right that a new theoretical debate, between the applicability of the concepts of 'fascism' and of 'national-populism', has raged around the *Front National* in the same way that the debate about 'fascism' and 'conservatism' has raged around the inter-war Right. Jim Wolfreys crystallises the flaws in such attempts to 'compartmentalise' the Right when he says, about the *Front national*:

> These flaws are fourfold. First, comparisons between the FN and fascism are based on a set of rigid criteria derived from a study of fully fledged fascist regimes. [...] Second, the FN is located within the national-populist tradition on the basis of naïve discourse analysis rather than empirical evidence relating to the organisation's structure, aims and origins. [...] Third, apart from a few vague references to 'the difficult gestation of post-industrial society' and 'post-materialism', studies of the FN make little attempt to situate the FN within the context of post-war society [...] Finally, the view that economic conservatism and fascism are incompatible has been undermined by recent studies of the extreme right in France.[7]

As Wolfreys points out, 'the FN shares a core of basic characteristics with inter-war fascism, and possesses others in embryonic form'. And, as we have seen, the French tradition of the radical Right fitted in to the 'fascist' tradition of the Thirties (despite the distinctions produced by Rémond and others), and there is therefore little point in pitting one against the other once more in a purely theoretical argument. Why therefore am I wary of describing the FN, and movements like it, as 'neo-fascist'?

It is above all because of the new vagueness surrounding the term, in popular usage. It is also because, unlike the Thirties, we no longer have the consensus, on the part of the 'radical Right' movements themselves, in claiming the term. The post-war situation has above all meant that mass support for movements of the extreme Right (as opposed to fractioned elements of street violence) can only occur if connections between those movements and 'fascism' or 'National Socialism' are played down. If this playing-down occurs, the way is open for support to be gained by tapping into current concerns, or national preoccupations. In all this, racism (in the form of reaction to fears of immigration and hatred of ethnic minorities) can play a major part, but so can many other issues where people wish to register a 'protest vote'. Though racism, and a good number of other issues, can seem to link these modern movements with pre-war 'fascism', the term 'neo-fascism' is a dangerous one. What *can* be agreed is that these movements share a number of the characteristics of the 'radical Right' in the inter-war period, and that to that extent, and to that extent only, they could, on a level playing-field, have been described as 'fascist', with much the same amount of ambiguity involved as there was in the Thirties.

1. Roberto Chiarini, 'The Italian Far Right: the Search for Legitimacy', in Cheles, Ferguson and Vaughan (eds.), *The Far Right in Western and Eastern Europe*, Longman 1995, p. 20.

2. Paul Preston, 'Populism and parasitism: the Falange and the Spanish Establishment 1939-1975', in Martin Blinkhorn (ed.) *Fascists and Conservatives*, p. 145.

3. Roger Eatwell, 'How to revise history (and influence people?), neo-fascist style', in *The Far Right in Western and Eastern Europe*, p. 310.

4. Luciano Cheles, '"Nostalgia dell'Avenire". The New Propaganda of the MSI between Tradition and Innovation', in Cheles, Ferguson and Vaughan (eds.), *Neo-Fascism in Europe*, Longman 1991, p. 43.

5. Roberto Chiarini, art. cit., p. 37.

6. Interview in *Der Spiegel*, No. 6, 1989, quoted in David Childs, 'The Far Right in Germany since 1945', in Cheles, Ferguson and Vaughan (eds.), *The Far Right in Western and Eastern Europe*, Longman 1995, p. 300.

7. Jim Wolfreys, 'Neither Right nor Left? Towards an integrated analysis of the Front National', in Atkin and Tallett (eds.), *The Right in France 1789-1997*, Tauris 1997, pp. 267-8.

Conclusion

'Libro e moschetto, fascista perfetto' (A book and a gun make a perfect Fascist), wrote Mussolini in a school textbook. Some of the reactions to fascism, in modern times, have been too concerned with the book, the written word, the theories of fascism, and have correspondingly lost touch to a certain extent with the lived experience, whether it be of the gun, of castor oil*, or of the alliances and perspectives of the moment.

By the time of World War Two, 'fascism' had, in most people's minds, become indistinguishable from Nazism. And, after the War, as the horrors of the Holocaust, and the depths of evil of which Nazism had been capable, became clear to all, there has grown up a popular tendency to dub everything we find distasteful as 'fascist'. Conversely, in the same period political scientists have tried, more urgently than ever before, to narrow down the definition of what was and is 'fascist' or 'non-fascist', to include some movements and exclude others, and to find new definitions for other forms of the 'extreme Right' which are then removed from the argument. More recently, a more healthy scepticism has begun to appear.

It may seem strange, in a book which deplores over-categorisation, to have tried to arrive at a 'definition' of fascism. The 'definition' to be found in this book is, however, a vague and elusive one, dependent on the circumstances of each movement at each turning-point of its existence. 'Fascism' has emerged as the term used, at a particular point in time, the Twenties, to describe one movement, in Italy, which encapsulated at that moment the trends and tendencies on the European right which had been developing since the late nineteenth century. The other movements based on these trends varied from country to country; and the problem for those who wish to define things

* Forcibly dosing their opponents with castor oil was one of the methods used by the Italian Fascists, and later by the Spanish Nationalists.

more closely is that they also varied according to their prospect of power. One and the same movement could stand for anti-capitalism, and for the support of the capitalist system, at different moments in time (and sometimes at the same time).

In this context, the old rejection of such movements as Action Française from consideration as part of this 'radical Right' has turned out to be completely mistaken, as the prominent part played by that movement in this book has shown. Various strands of the radical Right existed alongside Italian Fascism in the Twenties, including Action Française in France and the movements of the 'völkisch' tradition from which Nazism emerged in Germany. While some of those movements admired Italian Fascism, most did not see themselves, at that stage, as 'fascists'. It took the international situation of the early Thirties, and, paradoxically, the arrival of the *Nazis* in power, for the concept of 'international fascism' to be believed both by opponents and by supporters of the movements concerned; and, as so often happens, the belief eventually created the reality, as the whole of the dispersed 'radical Right' came to see itself as part of one great international movement.

In one sense, the unifying of Europe under the 'New Order' from 1940 onwards seemed to many indigenous fascists in the occupied countries to be the fulfilment of the ideals of 'international fascism'. But, just as the pre-war 'fascist' leaders who had come to power in their individual countries had had to jettison many of their apparently most firmly-held ideals (anti-capitalism, revolutionary change, destruction of the old elites), so these wartime 'collaborators' jettisoned what had been one of the most important ideals of their individual 'fascist' movements, namely nationalism.

So the close relationship between fascism and nationalism, which had seemed one of its defining tendencies, was lost in the war. In the post-war period, the word 'fascism' stood for treason, for betrayal of the nation. At the same time, because of the horrors of the Holocaust, the word 'fascism' came almost exclusively to stand for racism, persecution and genocide. And gradually, as a 'hate-word', it came into the generalised use we all know.

So, as they supposedly say all the time in Oxford, 'It all depends what you mean by ...' The word fascism has different meanings in different contexts, and for different people. From being a pejorative word in the mouths of its opponents in the Thirties, it has become a pejorative word for almost everyone. And the vagueness of the understanding of it does not matter, in one sense. It is a very handy word to use of what one disapproves of. We all make use of it, as a very useful form of shorthand.

The problem is that fascism is a more serious matter than that. Fascism produced some of the worst examples of human cruelty and horror ever to exist. It impinged on the lives of all who lived through the Thirties and Forties, whether they existed in the countries under fascist rule, or whether they eventually found themselves engaged in fighting a war to rid the world of this pest.

The rather academic question of the proper definition of 'fascism' fades into insignificance when we consider the necessity of constant vigilance, even in our own day, against the whole range of attitudes of the extreme Right that have been examined in this book. In that respect, it is important to have some idea of what lay behind these attitudes and activities in their heyday, so that we can be alive to the dangers as and when they occur. This book has endeavoured to give something of that picture, complicated and contradictory as it sometimes seems.

Glossary of Terms

Most terms are defined in the text itself (these definitions are marked in bold in the index).

Africanista. A member of the Spanish army who had served in Africa.

Anarchism. A movement of the extreme Left, basing itself on the principle that if mankind were not subject to the rule of law, a more perfect society could come into being. The means of attaining this goal included the disruption of the present society, often by acts of violence. This was, and is, an optimistic philosophy (as opposed to fascism), in that it presumes people to be naturally inclined to good, and needing no 'direction', whereas fascism presumes the need for the population to be directed by an élite.

Anarcho-syndicalism. 'Syndicalism' means the advocating of trades union policies (a 'syndicat' is a trade union, in French). Where most trades union politics has been concerned with activities, including strike action, which are aimed at the immediate amelioration of the situation of the workers, 'anarcho-syndicalism', created by the infiltration of anarchists into the syndicalist movement, was a movement which saw strike action as a political weapon in the creation of the necessary confusion which might bring about the regeneration of society. In the pre-First-World-War period, the anarcho-syndicalists formed the extreme revolutionary Left (a position usurped by the Communists after the War).

'Apparachik'. A compliant member of the Party apparatus (most commonly used of Communist Party members).

The 'blue flower' (p.116). The 'blaue Blume': a German Romantic image for the search for perfection, as described in Novalis's novel *Heinrich von Ofterdingen*.

Bonapartism. After the fall of the Second Empire in France in 1870, 'Bonapartism' was the creed of those who pined for the authoritarian but 'populist' attitudes of Napoleon III, in an apparently 'people-inspired' dictatorship based on frequent referenda which appealed to the 'people' over the heads of their elected representatives.

Boulangism. (See p.27). A movement formed in France during and after the attempted *coup d'état* by General Boulanger in 1889. Advocating as it did policies which appealed both to the workers and the Right, this was one of the first manifestations of the 'neither Right nor Left' movements which have been dubbed the 'radical Right'.

Cercle. Club. See 'Cercle Proudhon', 'Proudhon Club'.

Concordat. A political agreement between the Roman Catholic Church (the Holy See) and an individual State.

Comintern. The International Communist movement (in practice, the governing body of the USSR).

Gestapo. Short for Geheimstaatspolizei = State Secret Police.

Manicheism. A belief in the world as a battlefield between equal forces of Good and Evil, God and Satan.

SA. Short for Sturmabteilungen = shock units, or storm troopers. The Brownshirts. The paramilitary organisation which was the basis for Nazi power in the early days.

SFIO. Section Française de l'Internationale Ouvrière = French Section of the Workers' International. Founded in 1905, bringing together the many disparate socialist groups in France into one French Socialist Party.

SS. Short for Schutzstaffeln = protection squads. A special elite corps, originally formed as bodyguards for Hitler and the other Nazi leaders, but eventually becoming the major force in the maintenance of Nazi terror.

Venusberg. (p.116). The dwelling of Venus visited by Tannhäuser in Wagner's opera of that name.

Waffen-SS. = Weapon-SS. Elite military units on the SS model, forming part of the German army.

Walpurgis nights (p.116). The nights of infernal merriment, inhabited by witches and other hellish beings, on the mountain-tops of old Germany.

Bibliography

Atkin, Nicholas; and Tallett, Frank: *The Right in France 1789-1997*. London and New York, Tauris, 1997.

Authors Take Sides on the Spanish War. London, Lawrence and Wishart, 1937.

Barnes, James S.: *Fascism*. London, Home University Library, 1931.

Barrès, Maurice: *Scènes et doctrines du nationalisme*. Paris, 1902.

Bauerkämper, Arnd: *Die «radikale Rechte» in Grossbritannien*. Göttingen, Vandenhoeck & Ruprecht, 1991.

Blinkhorn, Martin (ed.): *Fascists and Conservatives*. London, Unwin Hyman, 1990.

Brasillach, Robert: *Les Sept Couleurs*. Paris, Plon, 1939.

Brasillach, Robert: *Notre Avant-guerre*. Paris, Plon, 1941.

Cheles, Luciano; Ferguson, Ronnie; and Vaughan, Michalina (eds.): *Neo-Fascism in Europe*. London and New York, Longman, 1991.

Cheles, Luciano; Ferguson, Ronnie; and Vaughan, Michalina (eds.): *The Far Right in Western and Eastern Europe* (2nd edition). London and New York, Longman, 1995.

Chilcott, Sir Warden: *Political Salvation, 1930-32*. London, 1932.

Delzell, Charles (ed.): *Mediterranean Fascism, 1919-1945*. London and New York, Harper and Row, 1970.

Drieu la Rochelle, Pierre: *Socialisme fasciste*. Paris, 1934

Drieu la Rochelle, Pierre: *Gilles*. Paris, Gallimard, 1939.

Drumont, Édouard: *La France juive*. Paris, 1886.

Eatwell, Roger: *Fascism: a History*. London, Vintage, 1996.

Gregor, A.J.: *The Ideology of Fascism: the Rationale of Totalitarianism*. London, Collier-Macmillan, 1969.

Griffin, Roger: *Fascism*. Oxford University Press, 1995.

Griffin, Roger (ed.): *International Fascism: Theories, Causes and the New Consensus*. London, Arnold, 1998.

Griffiths, Richard: *Fellow Travellers of the Right*: *British Enthusiasts for Nazi Germany 1933-39*. London, Constable, 1980.

Griffiths, Richard: *Patriotism Perverted*: *Captain Ramsay, the Right Club and British Anti-Semitism 1939-40*. London, Constable, 1998.

Griffiths, Richard: *Marshal Pétain*. Second edition. London, Constable, 1994.

Griffiths, Richard (ed.): *The Pen and the Sword*: *Right-wing Politics and Literary Innovation in the Twentieth Century*, London, Centre for Twentieth-Century Cultural Studies, 2000.

Harris, Geoffrey, and Wetherill, Michael (eds.): *Littérature et Révolutions en France*. Amsterdam, Rodopi, 1991.

Hibbert, Christopher: *Benito Mussolini*. London, 1962.

Holmes, Colin: *Anti-Semitism in British Society*. London, Arnold, 1979.

Jerrold, Douglas: *Georgian Adventure*. London, 1937.

Lasierra, R.; and Plumyène, J.: *Les fascismes français*. Paris, Seuil, 1963.

Massis, Henri: *Chefs*. Paris, Plon, 1939.

Milza, Pierre: *L'Italie fasciste devant l'opinion française 1920-1940*. Paris, Armand Colin (Collection Kiosque), 1967.

Milza, Pierre: *Les fascismes*. Paris, Seuil, 1991.

Milza, P.; and Bernstein, S.: *Dictionnaire historique des fascismes et du nazisme*. Brussels, 1992.

Mosse, George L.: *International Fascism*: *New Thoughts and New Approaches*. London, Sage, 1979.

Nietzsche, Friedrich: *Sämtliche Werke*. Stuttgart, Alfred Kroner Verlag, 1964.

Nolte, Ernst: *Three Faces of Fascism*. London, Weidenfeld and Nicolson, 1965.

Orlow, Dietrich: *The History of the Nazi Party* (2 vols.). London, David & Charles, 1971.

Ory, Pascal: *Les Collaborateurs 1940-45*. Paris, Seuil, 1976.

Petrie, Sir Charles: *Lords of the Inland Sea*. London, Right Book Club, 1937.

Rees, Philip: *Biographical Dictionary of the Extreme Right since 1890*. London and New York, Harvester Wheatsheaf, 1990.

Rémond, René: *La droite en France de la Première Restauration à la Cinquième République*. Paris, Aubier, 1963.

Rogger, Hans; and Weber, Eugen: *The European Right*: *A Historical Profile*. London, Weidenfeld and Nicolson, 1965.

Skidelsky, Robert: *Oswald Mosley*. London, Macmillan, 1975.

Sorel, Georges: *Réflexions sur la violence*. Paris, Rivière, 1908.

Soucy, Robert: *French Fascism*: *The First Wave, 1924-1933*. New Haven and London, Yale University Press, 1986.

Soucy, Robert: *French Fascism*: *The Second Wave, 1933-1939*. New Haven and London, Yale University Press, 1995.

Starkie, Walter: *The Waveless Plain*. London, 1938.

Sternhell, Zeev: *Maurice Barrès et le nationalisme français*. Paris, Presses de la fondation nationale des sciences politiques, 1972.

Sternhell, Zeev: *La droite révolutionnaire*: *Les origines françaises du fascisme 1885-1914*. Paris, Seuil, 1978.

Sternhell, Zeev: *Ni droite, ni gauche*: *L'idéologie fasciste en France*. Paris, Seuil, 1983. New revised edition, Paris, Seuil, 1987.

Thomas, Hugh: *The Spanish Civil War*. London, Eyre and Spottiswoode, 1961.

Thurlow, Richard: *Fascism in Britain*: *a History, 1989-1985*. Oxford, Basil Blackwell, 1987.

Weber, Eugen: *Action Française*, Stanford University Press, 1962. (French edition, *L'Action Française*, Paris, Stock, 1962).

Weber, Eugen: *Varieties of Fascism*. New York, Van Nostrand, 1964.

Winock, Michel: *Nationalisme, antisémitisme et fascisme en France*. Paris, Seuil, 1982.

Wolf, Dieter: *Die Doriot-Bewegung*: *Ein Beitrag zur Geschichte des französischen Faschismus*. Stuttgart, Deutsche Verlags-Anstalt, 1967.

Woolf, S.J. (ed.): *European Fascism*. London, Weidenfeld and Nicolson, 1968.

Zentner, Kurt: *Illustrierte Geschichte des Dritten Reiches*. Munich, 1965.

Index